Perspectives

Hadoffy

CONTENTS

Self

Perseverance

Spiritual

Pinnacles

Epilogue

Perspectives

- Hadoffy

A limit of existence.

Answers

Your existence is an unravelling chain of choices, actions and consequences. It will never end pleasantly. But, your existence must happen, and your choices must be made. If you stand out in a crowd and ask a stranger what to choose, or which way to go, or what will happen, their answers will reflect only the reality they have seen. *Their answers will reflect only their perspectives.* You too are bound by your perspectives. Under their limitations you will do what you do because you cannot do otherwise. And, unlike the you that is bound by your perspectives, they need not be bound by you. Within this book, a voice in the dark gives you answers. Answers you must question to refine your perspectives.

Aspects of Existence

Every existence is different. You hold a multi-dimensional, unique view of reality that no other can fully comprehend. This view that underpins your existence is all you have to play its game. At a different layer, however, all lives are the same—a brutal conflict between avoiding horror and achieving fulfilment. In the process of navigating this duality there are many aspects of your existence that stand to gain from an improved set of perspectives:

Your power — your ability to shift your reality into a shape that matches your desires, or denies your horrors.

Your judgement — your ability to make the right call for you at the right time when faced with decisions.

Your emotions — your feelings in response to controllable or uncontrollable, external and internal occurrences.

Your thoughts — your ability to free yourself from illusory constraints invented purely in your mind.

Vision of Reality

Perspectives change how you *see everything*. When you gain and integrate a new perspective, the sliver of truth that upholds your existence widens and sharpens. Your *sense of reality* strengthens and you become better equipped to play according to your own convictions. Improving your perspectives is counter-intuitively not purely about optimisation or success. Your best life cannot be determined within this existence. You have no means to compare this you with another you that chose another way, or any other being that was born into a different existence altogether. This obscurity is liberating. Your best choices will forever remain unknown. The optimal option then is to find greater perspectives. To not find them is to remain in a potentially grim and narrow reality void of the pinnacles that give life richness, where your choices are only shadows of their true potential.

Branches of Existence

With all of that in mind, this book is a broad collection of concepts divided amongst many branches of existence that will serve to expand your perspectives. These are not solutions for your best life. Nor are they hard rules or principles. There may be traces of wisdom and a weaving of art with science, but no perspective can be more than the sliver of vision it provides to better see the greater whole. Many sections will simply be reminders of a concept you once knew and time had made blurry. Others will be fresh and worthy of addition to your repertoire. Some will be disagreeable and serve as a counterpoint to the way you see reality. Acknowledging the perspectives you want to acknowledge and naturally forgetting others is an inevitable part of traversing the absurdity of your existence. In this you find your own answers.

Art of Perception

Unfortunately, with a great many perspectives comes a great many conflicts. Often it is impossible to see truth in full. Your ability to combine perspectives and resolve conflicting angles will come down to experience—practice in the art of perception. As your vision of reality expands and strengthens you might find yourself overwhelmed with possibility. This burden is a necessary downside, one that is paradoxically relieved by further improving your perspectives in all manner of contexts. When you learn this art, you start to see reality for what it is. You see that sometimes the voice in the dark is right. And sometimes it lacks perspective. You must think for yourself. What do you believe is *actually* true?

Path

- Unravelling the way -

"Metrics first, direction follows."

- Hadoffy

The path is best guided by measures meaningful to the self.

Metrics

What do you count as worthwhile? When the metrics you follow are left unchecked, you may find yourself pathing for years towards insane trade-offs or goals that have nothing in common with what you actually want. Blindly chasing the standard metrics of society—wealth, status, freedom and fame—will only lead to unnecessary suffering and angst. These standard metrics are not the issue. Their alignment with you, and only you, is what matters.

Drivers

Think deeply about what drives the metrics you so naturally pursue. Are they born of your own sense of reality, or are they a concoction of the people you are exposed to? Even if you identify the influences upon you, you, like all others, will struggle against your social conditioning, authority and needless comparisons.

Thresholds

Most metrics are infinite. Many of which are exercises in 'make number go up'. There will always be ways to push a measure further. However, diminishing returns will set a threshold for fulfilment, and raise the cost for acquiring less. More doesn't always mean better. You might chase excessive career advancement. It will cost you precious free time. You might chase an arbitrary number of investments. It will cost you the fear of loss. Be aware of your thresholds, and set them accordingly. Conversely, mentally setting a threshold too low out of fear or insecurity will rob you of the opportunity to feel a sense of accomplishment or fulfilment. Further, it will rob you of the runway to make progress, the vitality of life. Beware the comfort trap.

Uniqueness
Finding and pursuing your own unique metrics is not easy. Some of your greatest fears can be triggered in acknowledging the unconventional metrics that beckon to you. These metrics, often terrifying to push towards, are your most life-enriching options.

Curiosity
What do you as an individual find intrinsically valuable and interesting? Where does your mind wander when you are bored? Curiosity is a powerful guidance mechanism for finding worthwhile metrics. Do not corrupt yours with the agenda of others.

Contribution
What unique value can you offer the world or yourself? During your existence, there is richness to be offered and experiences to be had. At the end of your existence, there is a legacy to be left. When your metrics are rooted in your unique curiosity and ability to contribute, you will not scuttle by reacting to the world, you will shape it desirably by giving and taking value with agency.

"Valuable challenges supply fulfilment."

- Hadoffy

Problems worth solving, make a path worth travelling.

Boulders

What would it feel like to outplay gods? In Greek mythology, a mortal named Sisyphus is condemned to eternally push a boulder up a mountain, only to watch it roll back down. His endless struggle seems futile, yet Albert Camus in *The Myth of Sisyphus* declared, "The struggle itself towards the heights is enough to fill a man's heart. One must imagine Sisyphus happy." However... Sisyphus' problem can be solved if there are no special rules. Each time he reaches the top of the mountain, he can collect as much earth as he can carry and bring it to the bottom of the hill. Over time, he will flatten the mountain and eliminate the boulder's destination. By doing so, he'll have accomplished a task worthy of a god: erasing a mountain. He, eventually, would wish for it back.

Struggle

Your life challenges will fall into four categories. Survival, contribution, growth, and seemingly valueless ones, though rarely is a challenge a fruitless endeavour. Why should you seek these challenges, even when they seem endless? You may want people to look upon you in admiration. They might. You may want to feel a sense of unbalanced power. You might get to. You may want to transcend the system. If you do, the glory will fade in time. These results are not impossible, but they do not have longevity. The way an outcome makes you feel is unsustainable and never final. You may defy mediocrity through great outcomes, but you will still find your fulfilment fleeting. A singular spectacular fulfilling event will rarely outlast your lifetime. What you need is a constant supply. Having problems worth solving, solves this problem.

Problems Worth Solving

Being idle is the cause of many of your base level agitations and unease. Problems worth solving give your powerful mind something to devour. They are the only means to create stories worth telling and the only means to see how far you can go. While the outcomes of your challenges must propel you forward to be motivating and energising, the process of resolution paired with a sense of not wasting time will be what fulfils you alone.

Toughness

Sometimes you will not have a choice of which challenges befall you, only how you respond to them. Painful experiences, like heartbreak or loss, are growth opportunities. They demonstrate your resilience and expand your limits. The most critical reason to push through a painful problem or circumstance is to prove to yourself that you can. The more reference experiences you have, the more you see the limits to which you can operate, and the more invulnerable to difficulties you become. Beyond this, when you push yourself in situations where odds seem insurmountable, you get the fulfilling chance to see the full extent of your power.

"Man plans, and god laughs."

- Yiddish Expression

A completely predictable path is a boring one.

Chaos

You may not wish to live in interesting times, but in the current era, all times are interesting. It is precisely unpredictability that makes existence so exciting, and it is promptly the resultant chaos that can be so overwhelming. Once in a lifetime macro-level events are now more of a commonality than a rarity. So what does this mean for your individual visions and goals? Is it better to have a plan, or no plan? Why try control anything when the world is so brutal? If the pace of change of human reality is rapidly increasing, when does it become impossible to keep up? You have many choices. Among them, optimism and adaptation.

Adaptive Optimism

In the chaos of modern life, adaptive optimism is empowering. The adaptive optimist is someone with solid plans for a better life, who is also positioned to take advantage of the inevitable chaos this world so lavishly provides. The approach will depend on your personality and fulfilment metrics, yet is relatively simple. You construct visions and plans such that when the universe laughs, you laugh too. Even in times of bizarre adversity, you are either ready for, or have your expectations set, to weather the storm.

Planning

Plans do not have to be rigid. You should be flexible enough to pivot when reality deviates from your expectations, but you must not be so indefinite in your pursuits that you are tossed around in the sea of possibility, being unnecessarily prepared for nothing in particular. You do not adapt by abandoning all certainty. You must be both *definite* in your plans, and *free-flowing* in your execution.

Vision

Clarity of vision is vital. Whether you start with the big picture and work backward or build from small details forward, clarity anchors you amidst uncertainty. It is not about predicting every outcome but understanding the pieces needed to create the life you want. You need not rely on knowing every detail day one. You cannot.

Deviations

Life will interrupt your plans and visions at both macro and micro levels. Global events will shake the very foundations of your reality, and everyday mishaps will throw you temporarily off course. In these times, when plans derail, focus only on the present. You need only do what you can in the current moment.

Fantasies

A warning: do not let fantasies blind you to reality. Romanticised or wishful thinking will lead you into dark places, where the gods are made hysterical. Despite this, do not abandon your fantasies. Use them as motivation. Stay grounded. Trust your plan, embrace chaos and adapt. You will soon find your fantasy closer to reality.

"Artfully impose your desires on reality."

- Hadoffy

Master setups to direct the path.

Setups

Everything in life thrives with a proper setup. Your home, city and tools are all designed for efficiency and ease, but setups are not just about convenience. They are powerful devices that help you shape your reality, helping you tilt long-term odds in your favour.

The Tapestry

In your Norse Mythology reality is depicted as an endless tapestry weaved by the Norns. Imagine that you control the weaving of this tapestry. Your past weaves are fixed, but the future is yours to craft with the threads you hold in the present. Each thread represents resources—money, relationships, skills—used to create images that reflect your goals. The art lies in choosing and positioning these threads wisely, acknowledging that others are weaving alongside you, and may corrupt or enrich your images.

Setting up Setups

To build better setups, focus on choices with high potential value, rather than immediate short-term gains. These decisions will lead to the creation of richer images, which will create more unique threads. It is a compounding mechanism. Like selecting a job with growth opportunities over a higher-paying, stagnant role. The job with more growth is your setup into an even better job with even better growth or scaling. You setup your setups better this way.

Possibilities

It can take months or years to arrange your setups, sometimes in the order of decades. As your past builds, your future narrows. The hard part is seeing how the threads and their images come into play over time and what opportunity costs will be incurred. The better you are at narrowing possibilities to a desired point, while simultaneously preventing the loss of a future or other desire, the better you will be at imposing your desires on reality.

Precision

You do not need to create setups with perfect precision. You cannot. You also cannot guarantee that your victories will look the way they do upon arrival. They will evolve with time. You must accept that imposition is not always perfect, nor always possible. Variables, including others weaving their own setups, need only to be dealt with in reasonable approximation.

Art

Why be artful in your imposition? Artfulness provides the story or expressive element that drives you. It fuels motivation and turns your tasks into interesting stories. Setups, while constrained by science, are an art. Pieces are arranged, sometimes over long time periods, leaving traces and trails of your unique expression. This, brings richness into an otherwise dull objective path.

"Attention is overpowered. Pay it wisely."

- Hadoffy

The path reflects the subjective and is shifted by the objective.

Layers

Attention shapes your reality and drives your progress. It operates on two layers: perception (subjective) and progression (objective).

Focus

Consider how successful individuals focus on what objectively matters, or how gratitude shifts your view towards positivity. Like the expression "You are what you eat," what you focus on defines your world. Even in paradise, a negative mindset can create personal dystopia. However, the subjective is a choice. You can consciously direct your attention to that which is good in your reality, and give no energy to that which you deem negative. In this way, your focus will alter the way you see potential paths.

Attention

For tangible goals, attention is your greatest asset. Constrained by your finite existence, you have limited time for so many possible tasks. Your only natural leverage is to expend your attention with focus. Focused attention concentrates force, force multiplied, overwhelms. It is in this imbalanced proportioning of attention, that you progress your most important objectives.

Time Allocation

If an objective is important to you, you have no option but to give it a proportional time allocation. There can be no leniency. Your time is the most powerful and directly influential resource at your disposal because it is the only way your attention can be applied. There are two ways to improve time allocation. You must say no to anything that is not prioritised for your attention, and you must reduce the total number of options that compete for your time. Do the former daily as part of your discipline, and do the latter frequently as part of your evolving life strategy.

Time Utilisation

An old saying: *Some people count time, others make time count.* Time utilisation is how efficiently and effectively you prioritise and execute the activities you have allocated to accomplish your goals. Duration does not equal utilisation. You will rarely operate at your maximum. It too is directly influenced by your attention. To maximise utilisation: prioritise, practice, reduce parallel tasks, seize passive opportunities, prepare thoroughly, push yourself and maintain an open perspective. These simple principles will make all the difference in the return you get for time invested.

Deliberate Action

Mastering attention through deliberate time allocation and utilisation leads to deliberate action. Deliberate action is the driver of all progress and you must devote to it at all costs. Without it, you will not turn any of your great objectives into achievements.

> # "The level beyond is, until it isn't."
>
> ## - Hadoffy

The path has unknown limits.

Growth Patterns

Human potential appears limitless. You too will wish to break boundaries. You may wish to invent something new, improve what already exists, or elevate yourself through learning and growth. These options all fall under a number of growth patterns that you must understand over the long and short term to optimise efforts.

The Exponential: A slow start, but steep climb. This depicts consistent efforts resulting in low returns at first, then a major and rapid jump once certain conditions are met. A vertical line will represent a jump from nothing existing to something entirely new.

The Incremental: A linear climb. This depicts consistent efforts resulting in the same returns or same improvements over time. More effort can lead to a steeper curve, if it can be maintained.

The Logarithmic: A fast start, but diminishing climb. This depicts consistent effort resulting in diminishing returns or improvement over time. More effort will eventually be worth very little, but there are many areas where pushing this curve further can be worth it. Think of sports and feats of human physical achievement.

Mindset

Believing in uncapped progress keeps you from self-limitation. Even in finite games, the metrics that define 'the best' constantly evolve. Keep your mind open to growth to prevent stagnation.

Teachers

Learning from leaders, mentors, and peers is crucial. They both light the path forward and show you what is possible. You grow much faster when you do not have to expend energy or time learning the same lessons and trialing the same experiments as those before you. Never disregard the value of a great teacher.

Trailblazing

The best breakthroughs come from doing what has never been done before. Taking the lead and taking the world to a new level is possible, but assumed to be difficult. Sometimes, it does not need to be. There are many levers you can use to level up:

- Be creative and aware of nuance, originality is powerful.
- Embrace continuous learning, always be open to more.
- Find value in 'dumb' ideas, they spark creativity.
- Capture spontaneous thoughts, inspiration is sporadic.
- Seek disproportionate gains through unique strategies.
- Collaborate with visionaries and join others on their journey.
- Progress daily, even if progress is less than 1%.

The top is almost always an illusion. You may never know the next level until you are the one that takes it there.

> "Grand purpose is not predictable. It emerges from the chain of singular acts you choose in a lifetime."

- Hadoffy

The path is playful.

The Game of Life

Imagine an infinite grid of square cells, each either alive or dead. At each step, simple rules determine each cell's fate based on its neighbours. The only move that gets to be made, is the initial arrangement of the grid. This is the Game of Life, created by your mathematician John Conway in 1970. As the game plays out, complex, unpredictable patterns emerge. The fascinating part is that there is no algorithm that can tell you whether a pattern will ever appear on the board in the future. The only way to know how the game plays out, is to play it out.

Determinism

Much like the game of life, your life might follow patterns shaped by immutable laws responsible for the countless events that led to your existence. These laws of nature have played out since the initial arrangement of the universe and here you are, hanging on the edge of the next step. In a deterministic world, you are not to blame for your failures nor are you responsible for your victories. This can be freeing, or equally terrifying.

Destination

Whether you believe in determinism, fatalism, non-determinism or any other philosophy, the destination of your life is inevitable. If your purpose is not to simply reach your end, then the purpose of your path must be in its composition. The moments along your path that happen as you journey towards your end.

Intended Purpose

You must recognise that your actions always have intended purpose. Comparing life to a dance, each step in the composition of the dance has an intended purpose—a re-positioning, a gesture, a flow. Each is designed to evoke something in either the dancer, or the observers. The dance has no destination itself beyond its end, but the acts within have an emerging causal effect that send forth a chain reaction of consequence. Intended purposes, therefore, are all that you get to choose and act upon. This intention is playful in nature. Your visions and objectives can only be for survival or amusement when you cannot know the ultimate gravity of their outcomes and consequences.

Emergent Purpose

You cannot know your life purpose, nor can you hasten its arrival. It can only emerge naturally from your intended actions that play their eternal role in the chain reaction of innumerable causations and consequences that make up reality. Your legacies—your children, ideas, or stories—are all you get to send forth into a future you will never know nor experience. Their impact too will fade, but it can be beyond majestic to imagine everything you do sends forth a causal echo that permanently impacts the final shape of the universe. This final destination of the universe will forever remain a mystery. You gain nothing from knowing it beforehand. At most you can play out your path with intention.

Playing Well

The universe has laws. Laws you are obliged to follow. Reality will not give you the outcomes that you wish unless you comply with these physical, universal laws that govern you and all others. On your path however, you will encounter many rules. Rules that are flexible and ambiguous. Rules that sometimes don't need to be followed. And unlike the Game of Life you get more than one move. To play well then, depends on you understanding the rules and applying the paradigms you know in the contexts in which you need them. Beyond this, all you have to decide is what to do next, while there still is a next.

Performance

- Driving excellence -

"Max bets only."

- Hadoffy

Go all in.

The 'All in' Paradigm

To achieve true greatness, one approach is necessary: going all in. Winning in anything requires surpassing and outclassing all obstacles and competitors. You must exemplify unwavering commitment, unparalleled intensity, and meticulous preparation to fully go all in. This paradigm is high risk, high reward. Yet, it is the only true option to go beyond mediocrity.

Commitment

Commitment means decisively cutting off other options, accepting opportunity costs, and embracing the path chosen. It is about focusing energy, overcoming doubts, and pouring every effort into progress. You must be always on, ready to follow up and drive home any lagging tasks or derailments. While no stone can remain unturned and diligence with details matter, you should strive for completion within reason, sometimes sacrificing unreachable perfection. Resource commitment is equally vital. Hoarding resources out of fear stifles growth. History shows that many world-changing endeavours succeeded only because of bold resource investment. You may have no option to spare expense and if you truly have nothing to lose... bet everything.

Intensity

Intense effort, playing to the meta, and scalable goals push boundaries. Intensity is not just about working hard but working intelligently. In times of competition or seriousness, you must leverage the meta (most effective tactics available) for maximum effect or you will fall behind. It is the only way to know you did all you could with everything you could in the moments that it mattered. Intensity can come with imbalance. If you are balanced, you are at equilibrium. Not much changes in any direction. Imbalance is the only way to push beyond. When you operate with intensity, resource consumption may be high, but when you win at scale, outcomes and returns keep your efforts sustainable.

Preparation

Preparation supports going all in. Your British army's adage, "Proper Planning and Preparation Prevents Piss Poor Performance," holds true universally. Whether through training, system setups, or daily habits, preparation not only sustains your commitment and intensity, but minimises your risk of failure.

Go All The Way

In any endeavour, no matter how unserious, you only get out as much as you put in. If you are going to put the effort in anyway, you may as well do it right, all the way to the end. This remains necessary whether you are in combat, playing games or writing comedy. Committing to the bit, sacrificing everything, sometimes over a long period of time, is the only way to make it count.

"Slow is smooth, smooth is fast."

- Navy SEAL Mantra

Be agile.

The 'Agile' Paradigm

Rushing leads to costly mistakes. This cost can be time due to rework or it can be unnecessary expenditure of resources. Most gravely, this cost can be loss of life. The Navy SEAL mantra, "Slow is smooth, smooth is fast," teaches that deliberate, precise actions minimise errors. It is not about perfection but thoughtful execution. When you operate with near flawless agility, you adapt to your ever changing reality at minimal expense.

Precision

In high-risk situations, like weaving through traffic at speed, precision is critical. A rushed mistake could be life-threatening. This principle applies universally: combat, writing, sport, or business. Mastering timing and sequences is necessary. Deliberate and disciplined practice enhances both speed and precision over time. Even then, your fastest reactions may never be fast enough. You will rarely outperform a slower but more proactive operator executing smoothly with controlled emotions. Beware your emotions. They trigger hasty decisions, decreasing precision and increasing mistakes. A calm demeanour that does not frazzle will keep you attuned to what matters.

Fluidity & Adaptability

In urgent or chaotic scenarios, proactive planning and fluid adaptability outperform rushed reactions. You can apply the OODA loop model developed by US Air Force Colonel John Boyd to improve your ability to make rapid decisions and act on them.

- Observe the situation — what has changed, what matters?
- Orient yourself in the situation — what is your own status?
- Decide on what to do — what is the next play?
- Act on your decision — no questions. Do.

The faster you process the loop, the more rapidly you adapt to and finesse the situation. Having a strong understanding of the context will also greatly improve your ability to finesse it smoothly.

Finesse

Some moments are critical, others are valueless. Some levers are powerful, others do nothing. Some spots are weak and vulnerable, others are strong and impenetrable. Finesse is about identifying what actually matters and executing on it well. You only have a limited supply of energy, so spend it skilfully with finesse.

Take It Slow, Quickly

Frequent observation paired with deliberate and disciplined action is often undervalued, even in ambiguous and long-running scenarios. When you embrace the slow, you progress smooth, and because minimal avoidable mistakes are made, you are fast.

"Nothing to add here."

- Hadoffy

Simplify.

The 'Simple' Paradigm

There is valuable charm in simplicity. It is not about frivolously cutting corners or doing less. It is about clarity, concision and ease. Whether in life, products, or relationships, simplicity enhances understanding, communication, efficiency, and impact.

Simplification

Simplifying takes effort and is often harder to achieve than messy complexity. As Blaise Pascal once wrote, "If I had more time, I would have written a shorter letter." There are many ways you can do it well. Removing lingering problems or limiting the addition of new content are examples. You do not need to simplify in one hit. You can gradually make changes over time, improving clarity and ease slowly. Sometimes, a complex failure shows a better way.

Foundational Simplicity

Simplicity in foundations can greatly support the necessary complexity for you to achieve exceptional plans or outcomes. Consider construction items rooted in simplicity. Bricks, wires, concrete and pipes. Yet, with these and more basic materials, complex engineering marvels like sky scrapers are possible.

Clarity

- Filter information to what is relevant to the audience.
- Clear distractions that do not align with your goals.
- Ask the right questions to uncover the important truths.

Concision

- Use precise language and eliminate redundancy.
- Keep interactions focused and purposeful.
- Distil key messages into memorable, impactful statements.

Ease

- Remember that perfection is not always necessary, or possible.
- Simplify for others. To do this, understand them deeply.
- Question assumptions. They add unneeded impediments.
- Relax the problem by removing unnecessary constraints.
- Sometimes, solving a problem means removing it altogether by solving a greater one that encapsulates it.

Know When To Stop

It can be hard to know when enough is enough. Striving for simplicity can rapidly result in removing so much detail that all nuance or character is lost. In this way, one of the best secrets to simplicity… is just knowing when to stop.

"Who dares wins."

- SAS Motto

Be bold.

The 'Bold' Paradigm

While you may never face cataclysmic choices, fear will shape your life. It will drive you away from what you truly want. Your minor daily fears, exaggerated in your mind, will prevent you from taking life-changing opportunities. You will overestimate negative outcomes and underestimate your ability to handle them. You will use fear to protect you but it will also hold you back. Being bold is the only cure to this stressful and detrimental ailment.

Risk

Boldness does not mean recklessness. It is about calculated risk taking. Ask yourself: what is the worst that could happen? And how likely is it? Likelihood and consequence are easy to miscalculate. Most often, it is minor consequences exaggerated and judged pessimistically that keep you from getting more of what you want out of life. The real outcomes of your accidental failures are usually far less dire than you imagine. It is often when you feel that you lack something that you exaggerate the possible consequences for an action. Then, you overthink and convince yourself not to act. Adopting an abundance mindset—believing you have everything you need—is one of few counters to this paralysing mechanism. Beyond finding abundance, shrinking your problems and preparing to win will also elevate your confidence before you engage.

Reward

Rewards are powerful. You can leverage rewards heavily to counteract fear, especially in high-risk, high-reward scenarios. When you act on risky positions it is natural to sometimes come out on the wrong side. High performers do not just know how to manage the risk to reward ratio accurately, but also how to *recover* quickly and effectively when failures inevitably occur. Rewards can also drive a useful fear: regret. The fear of missing out, or the fear of losing what is to gain. This fear pushes you to do what you would not do otherwise and it is why it is so powerful to be clear on what you really desire. There is a downside though. The more you want something, the more you will think about losing it in action, which will further spike fear. It is a difficult practice to simultaneously desire something yet act with independence to the outcome. You must find the courage to do it anyway.

Courage

Courage is not the absence of fear. It is acting despite it. You must dare to act, not blindly, but with practiced courage. To do this, embrace discomfort and cultivate optimism. Hope and optimism is a potent force, sometimes the only one you have. With optimism, you can dare again and again. Beyond this, the thing you should fear most is never daring at all.

"A stitch in time saves nine."

- Thomas Fuller

Be proactive.

The 'Proactive' Paradigm

It only takes a tiny ember to cause a blaze. In life, destructive embers are everywhere within your processes, tools, and even yourself. These sparks can arise momentarily or linger, and once triggered, the chain reaction is hard to stop. Minimising embers before they disrupt your life and operations is critical. You will pay the price for rumination and hesitation. Proactivity is a must.

Prevention

Preventing a destructive ember of life from arising in the first place is the single best method you can employ. You will face many predictable problems in life. You will often fail to prepare for these seemingly obvious issues and suffer for it. Preparation is preventative. Have the right skills, resources and tools available to handle expected situations. You do not need to take this to the extremes. Consistent and well-thought out preparation will spare you from countless small impediments that keep you flustered, stifled and unable to gain momentum. Long-term setups matter too. Where you live, who you know, and the networks you build can prevent negative situations entirely by allowing you to impose only positive pathways before negative paths even arise.

Prioritisation

When preventing embers of life, it is useful to know the most valuable ones to prevent. You cannot stop everything before it happens. At some point prevention becomes too intrusive or obstructive that you will not progress if you try to control everything. Focus on the most critical areas instead, noting the Pareto Principle (80/20 rule): 20% of causes lead to 80% of consequences. By addressing that vital 20% first, you prevent the most impactful problems, without over-extending your efforts. Sometimes timing matters. Sometimes preventing cataclysmic consequences matters more. Sometimes a build up of similar embers causes a very specific problem. Prioritisation is not just about knowing which problems to address but also knowing those you will have to address consistently or habitually.

Control

When there are embers of life you cannot extinguish, all you can do is manage the risk and keep the embers away from catalysts and fuel. Control comes from your approach, patience, emotional regulation, and composure. Know when you need to act or hold back, manage your reactions to surprises, or stay grounded under pressure to keep embers from multiplying. Sometimes, doing nothing is the smartest move. Sometimes, intentional avoidance is the only valid option. With that said, proactivity is not just about avoiding disaster and annoyances. It is just as powerful for protecting, prioritising and controlling your positive chances too. When you are proactive, you unlock the possibility to snowball.

> "Stack your wins, find the exponent, capture your outcomes. Build your snowball."

> - Hadoffy

Snowball.

The 'Snowball' Paradigm

An avalanche starts with billions of tiny snowflakes, gathering over time until one trigger sets everything in unstoppable motion. Similarly, your efforts build momentum through consistent, small actions that stack your positives into unparalleled effects. Like building a snowball, each positive step compounds, giving you access to power spikes you may have never thought possible.

Compounding

In life, snowballing stacks tiny wins into massive successes. Recognising and stacking small positives creates exponential growth particularly when a feedback loop is in play. When the outputs of your activity can be fed back into the activity to make the relevant mechanism more powerful, you have an ideal scenario for compounding. Use these systems liberally. Beyond recognising feedback loops, you must learn to identify what counts as a tiny win. They are everywhere and can be especially difficult to find when you need them most, specifically when you are in a state of disarray and must recover. You will quickly feel a bad situation turn around when you seek small wins.

Momentum

When you are winning, do not let up. When you lose greatly, collect small positives to counteract the stagger. Momentum requires humility and relentless focus. Complacency breaks it. Discipline sustains it. Key moments matter for momentum. You might only get a short window to capture a small win. You might only get to decide once on a commitment before there is no turning back. You might only be able to capture a portion of the outputs of your activities. Know these moments, and do what you can to seize the opportunities while they exist.

Consistency

Compounding and momentum demand consistency. Whether in compounding finances, projects, or personal goals. You need to keep the pressure on and allow your positive outcomes to bolster each other. This applies to skills, habits and relationships too. Consistent effort will feed consistent growth, but only if you own and capture the fruits of your efforts. If you do not capture a meaningful portion of your outcomes, you will never have a way to harness the exponential powers of compounding, or trigger the threshold-breaking powers of momentum. Ownership is key.

Win by a Landslide

Be careful focusing on battles you should not be fighting. Others will have spent years building a snowball you could never compete with. Instead, invest in small wins over distractions, capture the value you generate, feed it back, and build your own.

"To go fast, go alone. To go far, go together."

- African Proverb

Cooperate.

The 'Cooperative' Paradigm

There are numerous challenges when working with others. You want to remove as many barriers between you, your allies, and your progress towards your shared objectives. You also want to be easy to work with, but you do not necessarily want to concede your individual power by being too agreeable. Knowing that you cannot do great things alone, consider the following:

- To perform well as a team, you must perform well as an individual. And,
- To perform well as an individual, you must perform well as a team.

The Individual

Cooperation starts with individual competence. Know your role, master the skills of your domain, and understand when to stick to your remit or branch out to assist. In this, trust is a necessity. It is built through reliability and mutual respect. Without trust, even the most skilled member can destroy the group. You must trust that your team is going to play their part, and then you need to play yours. Trust also enables autonomy, which minimises managerial overhead and leadership strain. Empowered individuals are far more effective and adaptive than when they are constrained by a micro-manager. You must also learn to appropriately share domain information. Precision and timeliness are key. You must have knowledge of what is, and is not, relevant to everyone else. This ensures the rest of the team sees the bigger picture without fluff, enabling informed decisions beyond your area of operation.

The Team

Your team can only thrive when the elements of chemistry, composition, and communication are aligned. Chemistry fosters synergy, while composition—diverse roles and skills—creates new capabilities. Above all, is the need for clear and concise communication.

Chemistry

Chemistry is a complex team function. It is the emotional, physical or psychological interaction between team members that is necessary for powerful synergies. For chemistry to build, you need to know individual competencies, behaviours and patterns. To have strong chemistry is to read each other perfectly, to act in combined harmony with synchronised, elevated power. If you do not have chemistry, or have negative chemistry, find a new team. Sometimes, you will not fit into the pack. Diversity of thought can be valuable, but should only be sought in alignment with chemistry. Otherwise, competing interests can break down the team functions that make diversity of thought useful. Do not blindly assume that your differences will complement each other.

Composition

Composition is a deceptively simple team function. It is the roles, resources or competencies held by the individuals of the team that may also allow for emergence of new capability. Finding an optimal team composition provides more options and better counters and is sometimes a condition for success. If you need, either adapt your own role, or find someone else to fill the gaps.

Communication

Communication is paramount. Clarity, concision, precision and accuracy. These are the necessary elements you must strive to get right in your messaging and methods, to allow for clear interpretation. Sometimes, even silence speaks optimally, allowing teammates the space to process and act without disruption. Your teams that embrace and reward calculated risks in an endeavour to win, will also find transparency comfortable and favourable. With transparency, information will circulate uninhibited, further snowballing the power of the collective.

Build a Pantheon

Ultimately, no team is perfect. Disagreements and unexpected challenges arise, but commitment to decisions—even amid dissent—is necessary to have any chance of progress. It is better to imagine yourself amongst a pantheon of powerful individuals with varying values to bear. It may take some time for you and others to come to power, but it will be these connected efforts that unlock your most life changing results.

Social

- Building connection -

"Emit positive energy, raise positive emotion."

- Hadoffy

The essence of connection is energy.

Infectious Energy

You know someone whose negativity casts a shadow. Their passive-aggressive complaints. Their scowls. Their victimising. They drain you of your will to exist. You also know someone that always lifts your spirits. Conversations feel effortless and cheerful, even their mere presence is enough to invigorate you. This is the power of social energy. It is contagious. Spread good energy.

Calibration

Emitting positive energy is not about forced positivity. It is about calibrating to the situation and acting with authenticity. Whether through playful banter, genuine excitement, or simple, heartfelt gestures, you can elevate almost every interaction if you act as a *source of contextually positive* energy. Even in tough times, like offering sincere condolences at a funeral, your supportive presence brings comfort and unity. Spend little time deliberating what is good energy for the context. *Feel it.*

Transference

You are not immune to the energy emitted by others. Negativity of others will drain you, while positivity will attract and uplift you. At all times transference is occurring between everyone in the dynamic, with some individuals having little effect, and others commanding the exchange. You will find grand gestures are rarely necessary. Transference happens continuously. Sometimes silence is key. Sometimes a playful joust is what elevates the dynamic. Sometimes chaos carries the upward climb. Above all though, is the need for authenticity. Fake enthusiasm or insincere flattery is easily spotted and has the opposite effect. The only thing worse than constant negativity, is false positivity.

State

Managing the energy you emit starts with managing your state. Managing your own state starts with small actions. Practice leaning your subjective thoughts towards a positive frame. The goal is not to see all things positively, but to keep yourself looking for reasons to stay in a good mood. This can be impossible. Even when you surround yourself with uplifting people and stack small wins, there can be times your mood does not shift. This is okay. Neutral expression or internal admittance that your state is suboptimal is natural. Ride out the present moment as you are.

Counterpoints

Not all positive social outcomes come from a positive transference of energy. Sometimes negativity must be emitted. Anger needs to be expressed. Concern needs to be shown. This is particularly true in romantic relationships. In the end, people remember how you make them feel more than anything else. So as the old expression goes: change their mood, not their mind.

"Never mind, all good."

- Hadoffy

Thinking is distracting, presence is engaging.

Lost in Thought

You have had many moments where your mind wanders, pulling you away from what is in front of you. You have been distracted, lost in thought, scarcely present. Your mind has raced with doubts about the future, it has locked in pondering a past mistake, it has been acutely conscious of your appearance. Caught up in your own mind, you have let bids for connection slip from your grasp.

The Powerful Mind

Your education teaches you to analyse critically, to break problems down with logic and to think objectively with data. The drawback of ruthless objectivity is the added propensity to analyse everything and anything, resulting in overthinking. Your powerful mind is exceptional at anxiety-inducing thought and self-criticism. Even to its own detriment. Sometimes you must skilfully abandon your logic to find peace and presence.

Presence

Unlike objective problems, social dynamics demand presence. A presence only possible when the mind is not stifled by its logical drivers. When you are stuck in self-focused thought, you are self-conscious, awkward, and distant. You fumble your words, overanalyse, and lose your ability to authentically express the thoughts and feelings that will lead to connection. This not only affects your confidence but also how others perceive you.

Engagement

You can learn to shift your powerful mind into a state more suitable for social engagement. Your ability to stay in the present may no longer be natural. Years of exposure to your culture or environment may have conditioned you to prioritise your past and future. Yet, you can still practice presence as a skill, and with repeated exercise, it grows stronger. Start by immersing yourself in moments. Shift focus from your internal chatter to the environment around you. Notice the details of the scene, the energy of the group, or the beckoning in someone's expression. Engagement is not about drowning out your thoughts, but redirecting your attention. When you focus on others with genuine curiosity, you naturally engage more meaningfully. Boldness helps, too. Let go of rigid filters, speak without calculation, and trust in the flow of how your mind wishes to intuitively express itself. Conversation is best when the mind is automatic.

Think Before You Speak, or Don't

It is an age old adage to think before you speak. This is true in matters of business and reputation, but only when long-term consequences are an actual reality. In matters of fun, your consequences are illusory, so be more ruthless with abandoning the stifling thoughts that are the true killers of connection.

"Behaviour leads, command it well."

- Hadoffy

Interaction is fuelled by physical action.

Physical Movement

Your body is a powerful tool, one that influences your mind and fuels your emotions. Instead of waiting for your nature to drive your emotions, you can generate them through movement. When you make the correct physical actions, you shift your mental state and break your hesitations. Whether it is through your posture, facial expressions, or simply walking around, physical actions build your emotional momentum. Yours, *and others.*

Emotional Catalysts

Think about joining friends late at an event. It is difficult to match their energy instantly. Without an intense catalyst, many emotions do not arrive immediately. They build over time. You can direct and escalate this mechanism by purposefully generating the right energy before, during, and after interactions. There are many ways to do this, but one of the most powerful is to use your behaviour—your physical movement—as a catalyst. Sometimes, no matter what physical actions you take, other background issues will be too overwhelming to allow momentum to build. It is important that you do not force momentum too harshly when deep rooted issues are driving your feelings. You must fix them first.

Influence

Your actions do not just influence you, they impact the whole group. Slouched posture dampens the mood. Lively movement lifts it up. You can shift the entire energy of a group simply by leading as an example. Your behaviours are more influential than words alone. Your positioning, stance, gestures, direction of attention and subtle movements all sub-communicate to others who you are and what you are feeling. Lean in to show interest, subtly mirror others to build comfort, and hold natural, relaxed movements to display confidence. These behavioural cues all culminate in a transference of energy that will propagate within and throughout the group, even if you are not the natural leader. When paired with a presence that is devoid of overthinking, your ability to shift the state of the group is amplified. Your resistance to those in the group that are projecting dampening influences is also heightened.

Securing Insecurity

Insecurity shows through physically reactive cues. Darting eyes, stiff posture, constant scanning for approval and validation. Learn to keenly observe this in others, but also break free from this by acting in ways that enforce the opposite. Actions make everything real. They do not let your thoughts conjure false consequences. When you act first, you can shape reality and respond to outcomes proactively, not succumb to others reactively. Particularly in matters of the physical, it is always better to act, than react.

"Surface only complements substance."

- Hadoffy

The physical is outshined by the non-physical.

Self Display

There is a line in the Tao Te Ching by Lao Tzu, "He is free from self-display, and therefore he shines." This timeless assertion reminds you that a positive outward appearance is best achieved naturally. The less desperate you are for it, the more it arrives.

Two Halves

While looking good and achieving outward success can boost your confidence, they are only part of the attention and expression equation. Greater social magnetism is found when your internal and external selves support each other. You must get both working in alignment to benefit fully. This dynamic is not simply about substance over surface or personality over appearance. The external self supports or degrades the internal self, and the internal self optimises or diminishes the external self. Your internal changes can catalyse external changes, and external changes can reinforce or invalidate internal changes.

Getting Sorted

Consider simple actions: completing a workout, dressing sharply, or ticking off life administration tasks. These small wins uplift your mood, and sometimes have a directly visible outcome externally. When you put effort into your goals, appearance, and personal growth, you also feel internally sorted. Confident, ready, and resilient. When you know you have done the work you needed to, you end up in a much better state for all situations. Get sorted.

Substance

Ensure your efforts align with and accentuate your genuine self and are not just an attempt to impress others. People can quickly detect when someone is focusing on the surface level without having the substance to back it up. You can see this mechanism play out when someone overtly describes or assigns a status to themselves, usually one that is delusional. To avoid this mistake, focus on progressing goals such that your status clearly emerges from your outcomes, lifestyle and reality, and is never a fragile projection of your spoken delusions.

Self Awareness

It is of utmost importance to be aware of, but not self-conscious of, both your internal and external self. Only then can you change and display yourself without an aura of lack or attention seeking desperation. Change can be hard. Your concept of 'you' can be ingrained so deeply that you may fear by changing things you will no longer recognise yourself. You may fall into the opposite camp. You may have no concept of your own identity, often resolving to act as a chameleon blending in with those around you. Ultimately, you are the one that must live with you as you are. Ask yourself, if you do not like yourself, can you expect others to like you too?

"Mask or no mask, what others perceive, matters."

- Hadoffy

Power is a matter of perception.

Tools

In every human interaction you have ever had, you have been confined to the limits of your perception. From subtle changes in facial expressions, to preceding reputations you have heard of, to first impressions that you refine over time, your perception is the primary social navigation tool used by you and everyone you have ever known.

Means to Power

The perception others have of you is a powerful lever you will use. While you cannot control every aspect of the way you are perceived, you can influence it to your advantage. When you understand how you are seen and how to shape that image, you can position yourself in any way you deem fit.

Warnings

Controlling the ways you are perceived is a double edged sword. Your logic of cause and effect can be woefully flawed, partially due to the subjective nature of existence and the limits of your lived experience. When you put on a mask, expect mixed results.

Aspects of Perception

There are many aspects to understand for controlling perceptions:

Resonance — The way you relate to others. It is not just about having similar interests or values. It can be about how you make others feel by behaving the way you do in situations or how you present externally. Overly curated individuals are rarely relatable.

Subjectivity — Everyone perceives everything through their own, often poorly tuned filters. It will never be possible to please everyone. So don't. Casting too wide a net will keep you generic.

Expectations — Credibility and beliefs stem from your status and presentation. Use these assumptions to your benefit. Embrace perceived weaknesses to surprise and excel when it counts. Align with contexts to earn trust faster. As an example, a very fit personal trainer or sharp lawyer aligns with their context well.

Proofing — Visibility of popularity can amplify influence. When paired with genuine connections, you effortlessly appear worthy.

Self Perception

The perception game is fragile and mastering it begins with self-perception. And, your self perception will ultimately be self-fulfilling. But, even you are not immune to your own masks. It is impossible to reliably control the way you are perceived if you cannot bring yourself to see yourself truthfully—mask on *or* off.

"Be a buff, not a curse. Nice lies rarely do favours."

- Hadoffy

The truth is difficult to tell, impossible to retract, critical for trust.

True Friends Stab You in the Front

Honesty is one of life's greatest challenges. Yet, it is a critical element of trust. There are countless scenarios where telling the truth risks hurting you or your relationships in the immediate term. But, while telling the truth can be hard, its long term value is greater than the temporary comfort of a lie. If you wish to build trust, tough truths told kindly are the most sturdy building blocks.

Transparency

In both personal and professional circles, transparent communication enables growth, stronger connection and optimised team play. Sharing your genuine thoughts with disclosure of your certainty, or uncertainty, helps your friends make informed decisions without undermining their agency. To not give them the perspective that they need, will keep them blind to helpful information and possibly set them up for failure. The choices of others however, are their own. Your role is to provide your view, not dictate decisions. In the process of being honest, do not come to expect others to act in the way you prescribe. Equally, you are not responsible for their choices either.

Pitfalls

Honest transparency accelerates problem-solving and enables information to flow where it needs but comes at the risk of exposing your own flaws or failures. This is particularly true in work. If transparency is not safe in your environment, seek out a culture where it is. When no one in the group can be safely honest without fear, you will suffer the repercussions of withheld or corrupted information. Sometimes, a 'need to know' rule is a necessary restriction for security. There are many situations where you must be a metaphorical vault and strictly contain the flow of information at all costs. Be infallible in this context.

Culture

You can be the driver of a culture where honesty becomes habitual and natural. It is simple. Do not punish allies or friends for exposing their own flaws in the practice of transparency. The benefits of information flow will be recognised by everyone, and positive results will incentivise further open behaviour. When you don't know what you don't know, this openness can save you.

Framing

Miscommunication often arises from assumptions. Whether in relationships or the workplace, having explicit clarity prevents misunderstandings. Further, healthy disagreements, grounded in openness, can lead to better solutions. The key lies in framing your messaging wisely. Target ideas, not people, and embrace humility, knowing there are limits to your own perspective.

"Reduce the pressure, but play with tension."

- Hadoffy

Ambiguity is unavoidable.

Rules

From the dawn of human interaction, all social conventions have been entirely made up. Across cultures and eras, rules emerged for various reasons, often contradicting and conflicting from one group to another. In tribal times, failing to fit in could mean exile— inevitable death. Today, you face an even more complex maze of social rules that are more nuanced and globally interconnected than ever before. Consequences of failure, however, are less dire.

Ambiguity

There is a liberating truth: no one knows all the rules. This ambiguity can cause anxiety, but it is also your greatest advantage. Social dynamics are fluid, and often, the pressures you feel are self-imposed, rooted in overestimating the importance of the unknown. Instead of fearing these grey areas, you can embrace them and use them. There are two ways to harness social ambiguity favourably:

1. Reduce the level of ambiguity and uncertainty that others feel, unless that ambiguity is favourable. And,
2. Act as though you are invulnerable to any sense of ambiguity.

Techniques

With the countless rules and contexts that underpin the different dynamics and groups you will encounter, there are many techniques to help manage ambiguity favourably:

Diminish Importance — Social interactions do not have to be perfect, nor do they have to fulfil a deep purpose. Personally reducing the threshold for what is or isn't acceptable to say or talk about nullifies the anxiety around saying anything at all.

Disarm — Do not punish yourself or others for making a minor social mistake. When judgement is contained, comfort is escalated and everyone feels more at ease. This disarming effect minimises defensive behaviour and allows others to relax.

Seek Common Ground — People connect over similarities. Never shutdown or shy away from clear commonalities. When you find those points early and quickly, you can build naturally from there.

Let Go — Not every issue is worth the energy. It can be easy to get emotionally caught up in arguments that have no benefit. Unless it provides entertainment for all parties, you are better off abandoning social battles that expend energy with no return.

Hold Tension — Not every issue should be abandoned immediately. Tension that stems from uncertainty, but is grounded in comfort, can be exciting and energising to keep in play.

Limit Needs — Enter interactions with minimal expectations and without the need for a return of any kind. Connections flourish without pressure and when you do not need anything, you are not placing others in a position to meet that need. Business connections operate differently, where both or all parties often have a need that can be satisfied by the other.

Test the Vibe — You do not need to be direct to test a dynamic. Statements with no agenda can reveal more about someones disposition than curated explicit questions. Sometimes starting out with something out of pocket helps elicit values you might naturally hide. If you value something, others often do too.

Show Intent — As a counter to the above, when you show intent upfront, you rapidly remove ambiguity from the equation and your tests will be more explicit. To balance forwardness, intent can be purely expressed through tonality and behaviour, not through words. Both context and time spent developing comfort matters, so choose your directness and expression of intent accordingly.

World Build — When you develop a shared imagined world with someone, any kind of tension can be created more safely, without the pressure of ambiguity going unresolved. This allows for in-jokes and layers to be built free of attachment to reality.

Default Option

No one really knows what's going on. If you are to follow a default social rule in all of your evolutions, let it be this: *Have fun.*

Self

- Conducting evolution -

> "A tomb now suffices him for whom the whole world was not sufficient."

- Plutarch (Life of Alexander)

Recognise the insatiable.

Pursuits

Throughout life, you will chase happiness, hedonism, stories, experiences, purpose, peace, suffering and meaning. These pursuits intertwine as you journey forward. Some fleeting, others deeply consuming. Despite your efforts, you will find that nothing seems to satisfy you permanently. Your desire for more will be relentless and your time in peace will always become unsettling.

Biochemistry

Dopamine, serotonin, cortisol, oxytocin. These are some of your great biochemical dictators that shape your every emotion and behaviour. You can understand them scientifically and shift them accordingly, but you will forever be at their whim. The aim is not to always logically beat them, but to learn to coordinate them.

Baselines

Your emotional baseline, or default state, is what you feel consistently without notable stimuli. Shifting this baseline higher is often seen as a life goal, but sustaining a perpetual heightened emotional state—like maximum happiness—is implausible.

Diminishing Returns

As you acclimate to greater baselines of specific emotional states, the effect of positive stimuli diminishes. Lavish lifestyles can dull the thrill of new gains, while small wins feel monumental when you are struggling. This relativity, combined with your brain's adaptation tendencies, are why emotional states driven by external sources fade and become harder to achieve over time. Hedonistic pleasures, driven by dopamine, follow a similar pattern. Over time, you need more stimulation to achieve the same level of pleasure. These insatiable pursuits, not limited to addictions, can become all-consuming, irresistible, and eventually unsatisfying. You will pursue them at your own risk, often to your detriment. And, you will never be permanently satisfied because you cannot be. You are insatiable by default. It is how you evolve.

Default Conditioning

When you were born, you had not overthought the concepts of happiness, ambition, peace or suffering. Those and your other feelings were just there. First they were tied to your environment, and then your sentience gave them meanings and associations. Soon after, others imposed their emotional patterns onto you, and you did so onto them. In any pattern, these default feelings serve a purpose. They aptly wire you for pursuit. No matter how much you evolve, how many goals you achieve, or what path you pick, you will always be in pursuit of something, anything. Do not try to deny this insatiable need to pursue. You cannot. All you can do is direct it, so it does not lead you down paths you cannot escape.

> "Blessed with agency over your figurative garden, it is imperative that you tend to it favourably."
>
> - Hadoffy

Curate the environment.

Gardens

Would you rather be a big fish in a small pond or a small fish in a big pond? This question carries much weight in the totality of your existence. Much like a flower in the wild, the environment in which you grow determines every aspect of your prosperity. Unlike the flower, however, you need not succumb to the unrestrained chaos of the wild. You have the agency to shape and change your figurative garden into an environment tailored to your benefit.

Genesis

All that you are exposed to matters greatly, but not every aspect of your environment is within your control. Your starting point depends on the choices of your parents, and early life offers you limited power and opportunity to change your surroundings. As you grow, past decisions and external factors will confine you and reduce your agency. These constraints are rarely permanent. When you learn and understand the elements of your environment, you gain a greater capacity for control. And, as you come into power, you unlock further options to manipulate.

Location

The geography, politics, laws, logistics and algorithms that you are exposed to shape your daily life and long term prospects. These are dependent on where you are physically *and* virtually. Every location will come with perceptible, and imperceptible, threats and boons. You may move for many reasons. Be cautious that the grass appears greener on the other side… until it's not.

People

The others in your environment are the societal lifeblood of a location. The people you allow in your garden will profoundly shift your values, standards, culture and choices, ultimately deciding your future. They will do so through many mechanisms of your own nature. The comparisons you make will motivate or distract. Your assumptions will be efficient or mislead. Your networks will create access or perpetuate drama. Choose people ruthlessly.

Abundance & Competition

The finite resources, energy and opportunities that you have access to are also the focus of others in your environment. These mechanisms present as trade-offs. Surplus and abundance eases life, but scarcity fosters resilience. Competition drives improvement and innovation, but too much can stifle progress.

Be the Gardener

Whether you pick the small pond or vast ocean, choose active curation over passive adaptation. Your evolution depends on it.

"In your duality of light and dark, do not stifle the dark, channel it."

- Hadoffy

Dance with devils, just don't become one.

Duality

Attributed to Aristotle is the quote, "Evil destroys even itself." To pretend that destructive forces do not exist in others and in the self is to weaken your defences against it. When you understand that everyone exists as a duality of dark and light, you can transform your destructive human impulses into constructive power. Not by resistance, but by integration.

Complementarity

Consider this line in the Tao Te Ching: "When people see things as beautiful, ugliness is created. When people see things as good, evil is created." Light and dark must exist together. When your darkness, often hidden or suppressed, is paired with the side of you that you show to the world, you gain access to untapped beneficial energy. Instead of subduing it, you must master it.

Indulgence

Society may label certain dark behaviours as vices, but these judgments often reflect personal biases, not truth. What matters is control, indulging in your darkness without letting it cause harm.

Fuel

Your darkness is necessary fuel for incredible achievement. Athletes, for example, often thrive under unconventional routines that outsiders would never understand. Consider the desire for vengeance. Unchecked, it's destructive. But channelled internally, it becomes fuel for growth. Redirecting the intense energy of vengeance towards personal goals will elevate you beyond the need for retribution. The key is in your results and self-awareness. Not every vice or destructive impulse can be converted into something beneficial. Some, like blatant alcoholism, bring only harm. But many darker drives, even those rooted in chaos like social drama, can be catalysts for success if harnessed correctly.

Flawed Insecurity

Insecurities are powerful motivators. They stem from your personal experiences, flaws, or traumas. Instead of allowing them to stifle you, you can direct them to excel by turning slights and disrespect into competitive drive. Not through rage, but controlled focus, by accepting, feeling, absorbing and orienting the emotion. Beyond this, recognising and accepting your flaws prevents you from being paralysed by them. When you do nothing, you are seemingly flawless, except you become nothing and no one. To better embrace your imperfections, remember that everyone has insecurities. What another targets is often a sign of their own weakness, not yours. When you shine a light on that weakness, it quickly reminds them that everyone looks better in the dark. So in matters of channeling darkness, better to not abandon your light.

> "The stealthiest killers of the self are doubts about the self held needlessly by the self."

- Hadoffy

Abandon limiting beliefs.

Efficacy

Your self-efficacy, or, your self-belief in your ability to achieve a goal, holds immense sway over your existence. Scientifically, high self-belief alone boosts performance, learning, motivation, and resilience. Ideally, it should be slightly above your reality. You benefit more when you believe you are slightly better than what you actually are because you do not readily submit to limitations. This resilience gives time for you to grow, which fosters further conviction and courage, often resulting in a higher probability of overcoming the problem ahead of you.

Silent Killers

Limiting beliefs silently hinder your potential. They sneak in through self-doubt, outdated perspectives and negative self-talk. Over time, they flatten your upward trajectory and can lead to depressing results. Intelligent people are especially vulnerable, using their intellect to rationalise the false limits they imagine. The remedy is awareness. By recognising and challenging your multi-faceted beliefs about the self, you are granted the opportunity to shatter them through real experiences.

Self-Talk

How do you speak to yourself? When mistakes happen, do you criticise, or motivate? Ridicule, or urge forward? Positive self-talk fuels confidence and resilience, while negativity drains energy and self-esteem. This is not an exercise in repeating surface-level positive affirmations. Positive self-talk is a deep and intense integration of words and emotion, both positive and negative. Sometimes, you need anger, rage or shame to give the words you tell yourself enough weight to be motivating and persisting.

Outdated Beliefs

When you are uncertain, you will impose limits to protect your ego, preferring the comfort of acceptance over discomfort of failure. This stifles growth. Your past beliefs and perspectives can come from a time when you were weak, resulting in learned hopelessness. To avoid this trap, you must continually reassess your boundaries and views. *You must always retest your power.*

Standards & Humility

You will harshly judge your weaknesses against the strengths of others. In this comparison, you will inevitably highlight your downfalls and lose sight of your advantages. As a human all skills can be learned, so your defence against comparison comes from setting high standards for your self and aiming for excellence. When combined with humility—acknowledging your current level and need for growth—all feelings of doubt will wane as long as you do the seemingly unpleasant: back yourself.

"Can't outrun the heart."

- Hadoffy

Don't settle; don't force.

Discomfort

You will feel uneasy when you go against your intuition. When you settle for what does not serve you or when you force paths that don't align with your desires. These dynamics feed off each other, creating cycles that are hard to break. When you force something, you often have to settle with the consequences. When you settle on something, you often have to force yourself to do things you don't want to do. Recognising the discomfort that comes from going against your intuition and perpetuating this cycle is critical. It is a signal from within urging you to resolve the dissonance.

Intuition

Your intuition sharpens as you experience more of your own reality. It guides you towards what appears to be the correct path for you, including the choices that will lead you through an endless sea of ambiguity and uncertainty. Along the way, fear and overthinking will cloud this instinct, especially when conflicting social pressures, societal influences and self expectations collide. Objective data will also play a necessary role but in this complex world it can never provide omniscience. Inevitably, your intuition will demand you to act one way or another. Obey it discerningly.

Calibrated Effort

In your endeavours, you will not settle on the extremes of failure or perfectionism. If you are to settle, you will settle somewhere on the line of mediocrity. You will barely suffer the difference between good and great but you will suffer greatly in knowing that you had the opportunity to do better and squandered it. Excellence then is not just about outcomes, but the integrity of your efforts too. Choosing to push, even if unnoticed by others, will build self-trust, an invaluable trait that helps to calibrate your intuition for effort. On the other side of this mechanic is the perils of overextension. When you fail to recognise moments where you are over-committing or doing more than is necessary out of fear of the pain of regret, you will suffer the consequence of unmet expectations. You will end up regretting the very discipline and effort you so forcefully applied at great cost for no reward. To avoid this trap, calibrate your intuition to as many perspectives and signals of the context as possible. This will help you avoid wasted effort.

Signals

A correctly obeyed intuition is one that is at peace in the long run. When your choices *feel* forced or hollow, take these discomforts as a sign to reassess what is causing the unease. Whether you stay out late when you would rather rest or hold onto a relationship out of some contrived fear, your heart will detect the signs that do not seem right for you. To better calibrate your intuition to improve its ability to give you correct signs, the words of Socrates are best but challenging to follow: "Know Thyself."

"Your character and your choices reflect each other. Deciding on one decides the future of the other."

- Hadoffy

Who, not what. Be, not do.

Freedoms

Everyone you have ever known will in some way decide who they are now and who they will be in the future. Some will blindly accept the fate that has befallen them and continue to do so, letting circumstances mercilessly dictate the person that they become. Others will meticulously craft the person that they think they want to be, potentially unable to satisfy an ever changing ambition. The former is free in that they feel no sense of drive towards a different self. The latter is free in that they do not fully succumb to the whims of random chance. In your choice then, remember that who you are, is far more important than what you are. Who you are, determines everything that you will ever do.

Historical Constraints

In deciding who you want to be, there is no obligation to cling to the past. However there are, invariably, points of no return in your life that will forever set in stone a part of who you are. These points in your backstory make up the series of positive and traumatic events that have shaped you. They will condition you one way or another, whether you intentionally address them or not. In order to change, the character you intend to become must therefore take into account the character you have been. Beyond this, your genetics will set some undeniable constraints, both physical and mental. Do not dwell too heavily on these. The future of who you wish to be remains mostly controllable if and only if you apply directed effort.

Embodiments

Life will loosely mirror fiction. Who you are in your narrative may embody the hero, guide, villain, or victim at different times. These embodiments will lead you into either pitfalls or benefits. The false victim suffering the most of the lot. Often, you will act as though you are a cocktail of the archetypes above, switching alignments as if you are unsure of who you must be. The key is to be aware and truthful of the current role you are playing right now in the very present. Only then can you decide if you are embodying that which you do not wish to be and seek avenues to change it.

Ultimate Self

Who do you ultimately want to be? This question is flawed. Curation of the self is perpetual. Your optimised and maximised self of tomorrow eventually becomes the imperfect self of today when any new experience changes who you wish to be. So while you only have limited chances to change who you are, it can sometimes be ideal to be light in your intentions and just let life play, accepting the flaws that will naturally arise in you. After all, characters are always best when they are genuine.

"There's only one way to find out."

- Common expression

Test for truth.

Testing

In life, the only way to truly know the outcome of something is to try it. Testing yourself—your beliefs, skills, and assumptions—against reality is the key to uncovering both internal and objective truths. The better you get at testing, the better you get at finding truth. The better you get at finding truth, the better you get at evolving accordingly. This is crucial for matters of the self, where your knowledge and understanding of who you really are, must not be stifled by your current view of reality.

Tests

Testing well requires both effort and courage. You must step into the arena of life and try everything you care about within reason. Across different life stages there will be different tests of relevance. The order, prioritisation, importance and type of test will be different for every individual. All tests will require you to ask the right questions. Some tests will be harder to unlock than others. Some tests will require you to just go all in and do whatever it is you are contemplating. Other tests will be blatantly thrust upon you, while some you will not realise are tests until the experience is over. All of these tests are necessary.

Building Evidence

Testing against reality helps you to build evidence of your abilities. This helps you build confidence, which helps you handle your fear when attempting harder and more rewarding tests. Your benefit from this sequence can compound rapidly but it all relies on one condition: you must actually execute the initial tests when they are their most difficult and fear-inducing. You cannot build confidence with thoughts alone. It can only be forged through action in the generation of reference experiences. Consider a doctor excelling in surgery but fearing a date. This discrepancy comes not from lack of capability but from lack of experience. The cure is repeated exposure to the scenario in question. Repeated testing of yourself in that exact situation. Each attempt at whatever it is you wish to do, success or failure, adds to your known set of experiences. Eventually, the unknowns and ambiguities that stifled your confidence become resolved and you adapt accordingly. Over time, with broad testing of the self, you will begin to build such an evidence base of your capabilities that it will carry you courageously but not arrogantly into unknown situations with new and ambiguous tests.

Elevating Difficulty

As you progress in your endeavours, you must raise the bar, confronting tougher challenges to accurately gauge and improve your abilities. This is not about boosting your ego. Increasing difficulty, especially to your limits, is the only way to learn nuances that comforting experiences will never provide.

Elevating Breadth

Whether through diverse friendships, travel, or unique roles, every experience tests and refines your perspective from infinite angles. When you test at breadth, many results will be singular and negative experiences. These are invaluable tests. They will tell you much about your dislikes and bring on realisations that go against your preconceptions. Sometimes you will not need to test further to be certain of your convictions. However, you must not finalise your testing too early out of fear. A singular experience at the surface level may not be adequate to find truth.

Endlessness

Testing is an endless endeavour. While you remain alive, the final version of yourself will not be settled. There will always be more to test and more secrets within your existence to discover. This endlessness can be overwhelming. Yet, the worst thing you can do is not test at all. You will find that regret stems more from fearful inaction than from missteps. Some people will be too ashamed to face even a single rejection or failure. They will suffer great agony in their stifled existence. You must test with perseverance. It is the only way to find the truths that will evolve you.

Perseverance

- Striving for ascension -

"You will be your own demise."

- Hadoffy

You are your greatest enemy.

Distractions

Your life is flooded with distraction. An overwhelm of choice and entertainment interjects at every moment. Dominated by technology, your day involves countless dopamine rectangles vying for your attention, supplying an endless stream of consumable content. You will tell yourself that you can be free of these diversions at any time. But can you?

Master Yourself

Self-mastery is the hardest skill to maintain. It is about controlling your mind amidst endless disturbances. Some of which are meticulously designed to capture your attention. Some of which are diversions driven by your biochemistry—natural whims ubiquitous to all those living such as fear or boredom. Whether you fall to the former or give in to the latter, your goals will always suffer. Your long-term visions will be derailed by short-term temptations, many of the temptations being illusory comforts or mindless pockets you cannot even recall. Before you know it, time will have passed, and you will be no further than the day you started. To reclaim focus and control, you have no option but to defeat distractions and your whims. Your existence relies on it.

Mastering Yourself

I. Assume that it is always you as the driver of your demise. Unwavering responsibility and accountability will incentivise you to make the correct choices at the correct time.

II. Curate your schedule and life pattern ruthlessly. For some, rigidity and precision is the way. For others, flexibility and approximation is the way. Know which you are.

III. Restart, reset and refocus. To return to a blank canvas or a refreshed mind is to clear out the blockers of possibility and productivity. Clarity will ease your worries.

IV. Prime the physical, prime the chemical. Humans are fickle beasts, do what is necessary to feel the right way before engaging. Sometimes, you will be forced to run sub-optimally.

V. Momentum is key. One slip can scatter your efforts. Catch your mind when it wanders. Construct habits that reinforce consistency. Keep promises you make to you and others.

VI. Be relentless in effort, modesty and confidence. Do not fear high standards or insecurities, fear a lack of impulse control. In this pursuit, remember to let go of what you cannot control.

VII. Fight yourself less.

"You won't stop if only you start."

- Hadoffy

Revere the process.

Initiating

At times, it will be hard to tell if you love your work or are simply caught in a habit. You will see your efforts as both inspiring and imperfect, torn between two worlds of self-love and self-hate. Yet, the more you progress, the more you will press on, piece by piece, because building something is inherently rewarding. Progress, even in tiny increments, becomes addictive, a testament to the power of your consistency. Before all this, you will tell yourself that you don't need to start just yet. Start anyway.

Process

There is a common expression, "The reward is in the journey, not the destination." So it is with all matters of perseverance. If you revere your processes, you will tolerate suffering and accept drudgery with indifferent vigour. Outcome orientation will still matter. Your results are supplementary rewards to time spent in a satisfactory way. They are fundamental drivers of pursuit, if only your attachment to them is non-existent. And so, the survival of your goals depends entirely on your ability to sustain the process of reaching them. And beyond your ability to master yourself, revering the process will make this possible.

Getting it Done

I. Set up systems that prioritise action over endless planning. Daily, small wins compound over time. Even setbacks are part of forward momentum when handled appropriately.

II. Strive for improvement but do not base your motivation on the outcome of every experiment. Mastering the process takes time and not every effort yields immediate results.

III. Construct the process based on your strengths. Channel attention into tasks where you excel, remembering that effort does not always guarantee effectiveness. Regularly adjust.

IV. Not everything will be fun. Some parts of the process will be tedious, but essential. Find ways to push through these aspects, whether it be solitude or social interaction.

V. Progress is not always clean. Sometimes the journey will get messy. In these times, fear of failure will only breed procrastination. Focus on action to subdue the chaos.

VI. Take the work seriously and respect the grind. But, do not take yourself so seriously. You must be able to have the humility to adapt a process that does not serve you.

VII. Do not just chase the summit. Cherish the climb.

"Curiosity is a saviour. You endure most relentlessly when you have something to hold onto."

- Hadoffy

Find anchors.

Brutality

For most of human history, surviving horrors has been less fictional and more of a reality. Despite brutal conditions of existence, people have persisted through unfathomable hardships, driven by unique, sometimes quirky reasons. When life is ruthless beyond all expectation, you will question what choices brought you there, and then you will question why you should keep going. You will tell yourself that you cannot continue in your agony. You can.

Suffering

Manifesting in many ways, suffering can be temporary, sustained, invisible or silently endured. You may not face brutal suffering unless you have been directly exposed to war, extreme poverty, illness or other severe and extended circumstances. But, even when winning, even when on the precipice of human living standards, even at the pinnacle of wealth and fun, there is struggle. Your agony is not rare. It is an individual experience shared by all, a potentially necessary evil to allow for good.

Enduring

I. Seek anchors. Reasons or purposes of any kind to keep going. When you link your continued existence to an anchor, you give yourself a basis on which to persist.

II. Anchors can be visions, desires or ideals that fuel your endurance. They can be situational, tied to fleeting goals. They can be lifelong, deeply rooted in your ambition.

III. Strong anchors diminish fear and inspire resilience, unaffected by the chaos of life. Fragile anchors that rely on changeable factors like wealth, are at risk of collapse.

IV. To find your anchors, reflect deeply. What drives you? What is *worth* enduring pain for? Once identified, do not weaken them with nihilism, pessimism or a victim mentality.

V. Strengthen anchors. Your reasons and purposes will grow as you do. The more you face suffering and surpass it, perhaps in humour, the more resilient and insensitive you will become.

VI. Anchors need not be grounded in the constraints of reality. This can be a longing for something that is so out of reach that getting there would be a miracle in its own right.

VII. If for nothing else, keep going just to see what happens.

"Everything, always, at all times, is a trade."

- Hadoffy

Cost is inevitable, do not be consumed by it.

Sacrifices

Every choice you make is a trade. If you had endless time and infinite resources, you would master everything without sacrifice. But, limitations demand decisions. The obviousness that your time and resources are finite will elude you, and navigating your trade-offs is not simple. Outcomes are never perfectly predictable and can be entirely personal. Further, the ambiguous sacrifices to achieve your greatest desires are usually greater than what you are willing to give. You can live with that, can't you?

Costs

Not all trades are what they seem. Ever come across something too good to be true? When dealing with a trade that seems like it was crafted by a demon, its offer will appear so tempting that it can be hard to know if there are even any downsides. Just remember, there is always a cost, and that cost is usually hidden in the long run, written in the fine print or masked in a well crafted technicality. This is why the long-term is the most difficult to navigate. Your short-term trades can lead you into circumstances you never actually wanted. Thus beware. Do not get lured by short-term promises and rewards that seem impossible to resist.

Making Trades

I. Understand your trades. What is the effort versus reward?
    What is the opportunity cost? What could you do instead?
    Does the public matter in this offering, or do they not?

II. Aim for maximum reward with minimal effort: low-effort, high-
    reward opportunities are invaluable. High-effort, high-reward
    can be worth it. Avoid high-effort, low-reward distractions.

III. Seek win-win scenarios. They make outcomes matter less.
     When you are forced into a lose-lose, outcomes matter more
     because you must minimise downsides.

IV. Beware of illusions and delusions. Chasing impossible goals
    can lead to regret. The chase for the impossible may provide
    progress, but be wary of unrecoverable costs.

V. Do not exhaust yourself with trivial and low value pursuits.
    Prioritise substantial and sustainable gains while recognising
    that your short term fears may cloud your long-term judgment.

VI. Respect the cost of gambles. High-risk high-reward trades
    can be irreversible and sometimes tied to pure luck. If you are
    to make these trades, be willing to accept the downside.

VII. In a world of endless optionality, liberate yourself with limits.

"Sometimes things just go to shit."

- Hadoffy

Adversity forges resilience.

Countering Misfortune

Whether you want it or not, your existence will inevitably involve bad luck and disasters that you must overcome. Your only counter is to forge the strength and resilience such that it does not matter what is forced upon you. This forging happens best in the brutal times. And sometimes, things just happen that are well and truly beyond fucked, that the only way through is forward.

Random Hardship

Many of your adversities will occur at random, appearing out of no where with no warning. Life will not ask you for permission and is not obliged to favour you or your wishes. There will be times where you will not be shown mercy or kindness in succession. One hardship will present after another, sometimes many will present all at once. When you face and surmount these unexpected and relentless challenges, you are gifted the knowledge that you can persist, that you can overcome. Remember too that you are not alone in your hardship. It may appear to you that some are immune to disaster. But, their adversities have likely occurred far earlier than you know, or are yet to come. Every existence is plagued with random difficulty.

Forging Resilience

I.   You are designed to struggle. It is in your nature to find a way through, even when probabilities seem impossible. Do not fear the inevitable, you have what is needed to succeed.

II.   Avoid the trap of comfort. It is through harsh reality that all life evolves. Those not yet blessed by adversity are fragile, lacking the evidence of their own resilience.

III.   Pain is a necessity in all things. There are pains that hurt and pains that change. You must be willing to experience pain, random or chosen, to progress. Immerse in it always.

IV.   Be rid of the 'why me' mentality. You will be a victim of circumstance eventually. If it does not lead to your end, it is merely a set back or grievance. Take the time to recover.

V.   Let go of the past. You need not forgive, you need not forget, but you must release the burden on your mind. It is a self-induced hell to dwell on injustices you can no longer amend.

VI.   Everything is unveiled in the moments of truth. Your weaknesses are highlighted and you get clarity on the changes you must make. Embrace the unexpected.

VII.   In tragedy, train your soul against the chaos of existence.

"You can't end on a win."

- Hadoffy

Most failures are a conditional finality.

Patient Relentlessness

In life you will come up short again and again. To surrender while progressing is to quit too soon. Patience with your accumulating failures is the way through. Only in relentless calibration and learning, acclimatisation and adjustment, will you find the solution. Sometimes odds for success will become improbable and you will need to reset. Sometimes failures come down to an individual not pulling their weight. Sometimes it is your team making a multitude of mistakes. Assuming you and everyone you need persists, slowly but surely, a rhythm will be found and success will be inevitable. If the context allows, eventually with enough failed attempts, reflections and adaptations, you will get it done.

Conditionals

When you are relentless, emotions will be strained and you will grow tired. Yet, for all of your endeavours, you will find that there are only three conditions where you fail completely:

1. When you *eternally* run out of time,
2. When you *permanently* decide to stop trying, and,
3. When the scenario *truly* offers no second chances (combat).

Becoming Unrelenting

I. You will never be perfect, but you can strive for perfection. It takes time to develop skills, it takes time to beat the odds. Only with time and consistency can you chase perfection.

II. Volume, volume, volume. Reps, reps, reps. Quantity is your way to quality and progress. The requirement for improvement is far more than expected. Everything comes back to math.

III. Your ego will attempt to protect you from facing failure. Brave the uneasiness of observing yourself exhibiting weakness or reaching limitations. Exposure to humiliation is a necessity.

IV. Do not avoid failure for favourable perception. A facade of success or experience falls quickly to any real test. Humility in all forms, backed by a focus on growth, will carry you further.

V. Nothing can outclass a high learning rate. A high volume of learning, combined with unparalleled experience, will surpass any level of untrained talent. Seek learning in all its variance.

VI. Focus, attention, awareness. Relentlessness demands all forms of your perception at all times. It demands it to the very end. Until success is finalised, there is always more to do.

VII. Success is also a conditional finality. It ends when you let up.

"Prioritisation, above all."

- Hadoffy

Focus on the next step.

The Sequence

To reach death, first one must be born. It is a matter of priority. Your existence is a linear sequence whether you control it or not. You may plan to the end and think of the end, but action remains confined to the very next step in the sequence. You cannot do more than what you can do right now. Do not overthink, do not hesitate, the next step in your sequence has already arrived.

Achievement

Every achievement is bound to the sequence. For you to achieve anything you must seek the next step of highest importance for your goals of greatest importance. Opportunity costs will demand prioritisation. Conditional pathways will open and close as available steps present and fade with time, but nothing beyond you can execute the next step for you. To delay a great step is to risk its existence. You also cannot process hundreds of steps all at once. Your ability to run in parallel is bound by your ability to initiate and coordinate each task in step. What you can handle is the sequence that progresses your existence. And, by reducing unfathomable chunks into manageable steps for prioritised execution, your grand achievements become possible.

Mastering the Sequence

I.   Everything burns steps. Reduce your possible alternatives to the most important alternatives. Cull options and steps of insignificance ruthlessly. Cull tasks, cull goals.

II. Parallel progression is expensive. Avoid multi-tasking and aim to narrow your focus to concentrate intensity on steps of relevance. There is much to gain when you single task.

III. The order of priority determines all success and failure. You must understand what must happen in what order. It will not always be clear, but it will always be critical.

IV. Steps will pass anyway. A missed step today, only delays the chance for progress to tomorrow. First steps can be easy. Taking steps in perpetuity until the goal is reached, is hard.

V.   Do not get lost in the steps. You may be far behind where you think you need to be, or far beyond. Be aware of your delays, but also take note of how far you have come.

VI. Remain curious. When the next best step does not unveil itself, you must seek new angles and perspectives. The next step may even be to abandon your current self.

VII. Do not resist reality. Step towards your preferred reality.

Pathways

When viewed from the beginning, the sequence of your existence is more like an endless branching pathway. Many steps you take in life will be choices made into action. Choices that forever solidify the possibilities of your future. Sometimes, the sequence of your existence presents unique shortcuts, hidden pathways to specific results either much earlier in your possible timeline or unique to the pathway itself. These pathways can be extremely abnormal, but with the right priorities they are not an impossibility. Finding the priorities that will get you there in time can take a lot of work in itself. A lot of executed steps. No matter what you do however, and beyond these shortcuts, the branching pathways of your existence will eventually demand selection.

Selection

To attempt to travel any pathway then, first one must make choices. Where your choices will actually take you… is a matter of the intangible.

Spiritual

- Harnessing the intangible -

"For every action you take, the gods demand another."

- Hadoffy

Change ever looms.

Perpetuity

History is just a series of things happening one after another. It is a fluctuation of blood and glitter that relentlessly unravels with each ending leading to a new beginning. It does not matter what you do, what plan you execute flawlessly, what desire you achieve or what materials you acquire, you will always eventually ask the question: 'What's next?'

And there will always be an answer.

Permanent Impermanence

In times of monotony your soul yearns for possibility. Yet, when change and opportunity inevitably arrives, you will grow anxious It is in this duality that the human spirit struggles. Your want for possibility ever conflicts with your need for stability. To alleviate this conflict, you must learn to accept a truth of reality: the only permanency, is the lack of permanency. In accepting this maxim you will find great optimism in excitement and great pessimism in fear. When you understand this inevitability of change, you can readily use it to your advantage for matters of anticipation.

Anticipation

If the past you no longer control is already written, and the future rapidly joins it in its finality, what benefit is there in looking forwards in anxiety? It is far better to greet the future in excited anticipation, ready to perform and control the controllable, than to meet it in fearful anxiousness, weak and relinquishing all control to chance. Nerves of excitement are a greater blessing.

Fear Versus Excitement

In your anticipation, you will face many fears. The fear of missing out, the fear of regression, or the fear of running out of time. But, are you afraid of missing a specific opportunity, or just the unknown? The events of your existence, though unique, are often repeatable. Anxieties fade when you understand that what you miss today can often be found again tomorrow. Excitement then, is the counter to your fear. The excitement of a new life chapter, excitement of new beginnings or the excitement of progression.

Fleeting Everything

A world driven by permanent impermanence is and always will be messy and chaotic. It is natural to feel the anxiety that stems from being unable to predict the outcome of uncontrollable forces that menace throughout the world. Just remember that because something is the way it is now, it does not mean it will always be that way. When times are tough, you will find solace in knowing they are temporary. When times are good, be aware of their fleeting nature. These fleeting moments, you must savour.

"It is a divine thing, to experience one's self."

- Hadoffy

Inner transcendence, outer ascendance.

Awe

Many things inspire awe. Grandeur. Intricate detail. Events so improbable they seem fictitious. In awe you are reminded of a world beyond your own, of powers beyond your control and understanding. It will make you feel both connected to something greater, and so very insignificant. Yet, here you are, a miracle of a biological creature, existing in your tiny pocket of time, in your little corner of the universe. Despite your apparent irrelevance, your human spirit needs not an external brilliance to find awe. You have an infinite and always available source of awe within you, and there is more than one way to experience it. With its mastery, comes the power to go beyond a prior self.

The Present Self: Flow

In the present, you will find awe through flow—full immersion in your activity, perpetuated by focus and smooth intensity. Being in this state of experience is divine. Time passes effortlessly, you feel a persisting sense of fulfilment and your power is unmatched. When in flow, intuition takes over. You no longer need a script and your thoughts are automatic. Only significant intrusions can separate you from this state. It can take time and the ruthless elimination of distractions to enter flow, but your ability to sustain and consistently re-enter it will determine many of the outcomes of your existence. Many of which you will reflect upon in awe.

The Past Self: Reflection

When you revisit your past you re-experience your emotions, actions and outcomes. This can be a terrifying reality to examine. You will see how your actions did not always align with what you were thinking and feeling. You will see how your lack of skill or perspective caused you to miss an opportunity or fumble a scenario. You will see how your emotions clouded your judgement and caused you to react in a way that triggered an unrecoverable downfall. To be able to mentally replay your existence like this is both painful and inspiring, but you will learn much: Why you did what you did. How your failures shaped you. The very small number of truly impactful events in your life. Reflection will clarify your values, inspire gratitude, and help you manage your flaws and strengths. Without it, you will never ascend in your existence.

The Actualised Self: Ascendancy

Experiencing your actualised self is profound. It can be likened to being on the other side of your dreams. When you realise you have accomplished a life goal, you will look back at the path and the moments contained within. You will experience yourself. This is not a purely conscious reflection. It is a feeling. It is everything that got you there, bundled up into a sensation. A feeling of ascendancy. This sensation will be your greatest experience of awe. The feeling that you have *moved beyond a prior self*.

"To better judge the probabilistic, observe the intrinsic."

- Hadoffy

Nature over form.

Natures

Have you ever known someone so well that you can almost guess what they're going to do before they do it? Did you know that some types of bamboo have a higher tensile strength than some steels? Two disjoint questions, but both are about something you cannot physically see: the intrinsic. Whether it be materials, people or anything else in reality, the essence of a thing, not the appearance of a thing, is what matters. When you learn to understand natures, or the intrinsic, you will begin to understand not just your current existence, but much of what might yet come in the future.

Context

When you observe what a person does, based on the person you know them to be, it can make a lot of sense as to what patterns they assume and what choices they will make. However, the nature of a context influences the nature of everything else. In matters of low consequence, people will act on their leisurely nature. In matters of severity, people will act on their intense or survival nature. The context of relevance is not always easy to identify and there can multiple competing layers and variables. These layers of context are what lead to both expected and surprising patterns, some of which seem contradictory. Think about how a soldier, conditioned to thrive under combat stress, may suffer from the uncertainty of illogical corporate ambiguity when they change roles. Thus, in all endeavours of understanding natures, you must not just look at the dominant nature of the thing, but the ever-changing contexts in which that thing exists.

Foresight

To change your nature is to change your destiny. Its power over your long-term trajectory cannot be ignored. While your traits and skills evolve through growth and experience, your dominant nature will shape every choice, action and response in your existence. For you to counteract the downsides of your particular natures, you must first be able to identify what they are and where they may lead you. Outside of the religious context, the seven deadly sins of gluttony, lust, greed, sorrow, wrath, sloth and pride, are an interesting model for exploring how natures prone to vice may turn out in the long run. While some of your strongest natures may be unchangeable, you can still consciously do much to mitigate how often you succumb to your lesser self.

Limitations

Sometimes even the intrinsic will not give you useful answers to probabilistic questions. At the highest level, that is a nature of life. Your existence is limited, and no matter how well you understand the nature of a thing and its context, you cannot know everything.

"What can a flower know?"

- Hadoffy

Make an impossible perception check.

Flowers

When a flower exists within a garden, it knows the presence of the rain, the sun and nutritious soil, but cannot perceive or comprehend the footpath, the fence or a gnome. Yet, as a human, you know those things exist and the purpose behind them. Just because the flower cannot understand the gnome or what it is, it does not mean the gnome does not exist. Keeping this in mind, the question then becomes: what can a human know?

Sensors

The biological sensory system of a human is not perfect. Even with technological assistance, the human ability to perceive is not all-seeing. You can layer the augmented human sensory system into three tiers:

1. *The Biological* – What you naturally sense and process unassisted: sight, sound, smell, taste, touch.
2. *The Technological* – What you can sense and process with tools, including the tools humanity is yet to invent.
3. *The Divine* – What you cannot sense, measure or comprehend with any tool now and in the future.

The Unreal

The third tier is the complication. Even with your advanced mind, you are like a flower in a vast, cosmic garden, possibly blind to forces beyond your perception. Does that mean these forces do not exist? You will never know. Your inability to see or comprehend them does not disprove their potential for existence. Further, a flower cannot know what to do to gain the favour of a gardener. It can only exist as it does. Similarly, you cannot know which acts are of relevance beyond your perception. Nor can you know if your acts even influence what lies beyond at all.

Beyond

Consider the following:

- The vastness of the universe. Your planet's perfect conditions for life seem improbable yet you exist against those odds. Is this a matter of luck or design?
- Moments that feel like fate. Chance encounters, pivotal choices, all connected by an invisible string. How well can you see the immeasurable number of events that conspired to create the singular moment you just experienced?
- Paradoxes. Conflicting desires, choices, truths that never resolve. Are you able to hold the conflict?

Your experience with the beyond will be deeply personal. A divine influence may never provide guidance and you may never know your place in its world. Thus the question then becomes: does a flower really care to comprehend its gardener? No, it just adapts.

> "You learn best about how to change in clashes brought on by your actions or systematically imposed circumstances."

- Hadoffy

Conflict leads to valuable adaptations.

Survival

You have been thrust into a harsh world where your survival demands resourcefulness, strategy and resilience. Stripped of choice over your physical genetics and initial geography from the outset, you must compete for resources and forge alliances, all while facing the raw realities of betrayal, drama and bad luck. You have no choice in this matter, and neither does any living being. From the time that the first basic organisms consumed each other on the ocean floor, all life has been in an endless competition for dominance and prosperity. To improve the odds of winning this competition, humans developed tools and weapons for protection, then used those same defences to conquer. At each loap in technology the principle was the same. Adapt, or die.

The Human System

The most powerful thing you can do for the benefit of your existence is intimately understand the infinitely complex human system you exist within. This is maddening. Humanity has never faced the scale and complexity of the problems it has now. This has been true throughout all of human history. The most effective survival and governance mechanisms will always be changing. Despite this perpetual change, the struggle of existence does not. To hold claim to existence, to thrive, you must change too. In a system with imbalances, there will be injustices. Despite this lack of fairness, you must adapt ruthlessly. Or, change the system.

Adapting to the System

In this world every moment is a complex clash of individual incentives, values, desires and flawed natures. Such mechanics play out as an endless source of conflict, with alignment of all humans appearing seemingly impossible. The global best is likely to remain undefined, but you must still seek out your own best in the system. This need to adapt applies to every individual. Even at the pinnacle of power within the system, you are at its whims. How do you know when you need to adapt? Conflict. When you find an aspect of yourself incompatible with the systems you exist within, usually denoted by a downward trajectory in life progress or peace, you will find yourself incentivised to change. And you must perpetually, or you will face consequences. The alternative is harder to achieve, but more freeing if done correctly.

Changing the System

When you bring your ideas and innovations into the system, you create a conflict of your own making. The system must resolve this conflict—your intentions for the system must be evaluated. And, if and only if proven valuable, whether by truth, deception or contrived and unfair imbalance, the system will adapt to you.

"When the gods beckon, answer."

- Hadoffy

See and take chances.

Beckoning

There are many things you will despise. You will count yourself among them in the pain of witnessing yourself miss a window of great opportunity. A late recognition. A brief hesitation. A fear that says no while your mind and soul say yes. The gods will beckon you, put all of the pieces perfectly into place, and you will refuse. Your punishment is eternal. You will never know what could have been. To alleviate this unbearable agony you will tell yourself that you are better off because of it. This is rarely true. Letting go of what is not for you is one thing, to never accept the gifts of existence out of fear or lack of skill or experience, is another.

Awareness

You can never truly master the timing of life. Existence will always be in a state of flux between nothing happening at all, and everything happening at once. In both stagnation and chaos, there are always hidden and fleeting moments of chance. Seeing them is not easy. They come in many forms. Some change your course forever, others offer scenic detours to the same result. Some manifest over long periods of time, while others appear out of no discernible pattern at all. The more attuned you get to patterns and indicators, the more opportunities you will see. There are many ways to improve in your awareness of chances:

- Seek learning. Indulge in the experiment or test.
- Be curious. Follow the thread by letting something play out.
- Go out. Do what you set out to do. Chances will follow.
- Connect with people. They open more lanes to find chances.
- Notice the perfect storm, where everything comes together.

Action

Windows are small. Should you act now, or in a moment? Should you be patient, or urgent? The more you become aware of chances, the more you will see the windows within windows. The chances within chances within chances. These are the true tests, and there is no way to get it right every time. You must still act.

- Accept the gift. Capitalise on luck when it strikes, take the shot.
- Beware the false chance. The house eventually wins.
- Transcend fear. Do not debate or hesitate to your detriment.
- Have foresight. You can make timely preparations.
- Always have a round in the chamber. Chances strike suddenly.

Practice

See and take chances, over and over. Not to become needlessly opportunistic, but to see the opportunity in everything. You will find the true absurdity and richness of existence in this practice. As Mark Twain wrote, "Truth is stranger than fiction, but it is because fiction is obliged to stick to possibilities; Truth isn't."

"Consider the end."

- Scottish Clan Kennedy Motto

Endings are necessary.

Liberation

You live in a world liberated by endings. Lives. Friendships. Relationships. Pets. The sense of happiness. These are all things that can grow into horrors beyond your comprehension if they are never to meet their inevitable and necessary conclusions. When their endings are to arrive you may not know. Sometimes you will be the liberator—the actor that enforces conclusions. Some you may want. Some you may regret. It is of great fortune then that you, having faced countless endings in your lifetime, will eventually be freed by an ultimate ending of your own.

Death

Death is the greatest liberator. In death all feelings are annihilated, all thoughts muted, all chances to change are rescinded. You will perish with possibilities unresolved and answers unreceived. In time, your past will be swept away and your legacy will fade. Most people will never know you existed and the few that did will also cease to think of you. Knowing this, death becomes so powerful that it liberates you before it has even occurred. Remembering it, and the way it so ruthlessly permeates everything, will alleviate you to experience life for the insanity it is.

Self Death

You will die many times. Not literally, but many parts of your self and soul. Some parts of you that you will deem most important must perish for you to move forward. Sometimes you will need a different self for a different stage. Sometimes you will find an old self has already left you or that a part of yourself was built on a fantasy that must be let go. Sometimes a self death will be justified and sometimes the darkness of reality will hit you so deeply that your naivety dies with the innocent self that harboured it. Do not fear the self death, fear the consequences of resisting what is necessary. Be wary however, do not allow the good parts of the self to die needlessly. You need not let the horrors of existence turn you into a horror of your own kind too.

Loss & Enrichment

Things you will lose: Close Friends. Parents. Dream jobs. Games of no consequence. Your enthusiasm. Some of these things you will find anew, others you will find something similar, and others can never be replaced. In their existence you have gained: Memories. Lessons. The motivation to push forward. The insight to do what is right. Despite these gains, your pain from loss will not be gentle. You will be haunted by dead rituals. The morning coffee they'll never make you again. The inside jokes that will never be brought up at the most inappropriate of times. The toast before a shot to a singular expression of great meaning. While haunting, these memories permanently enrich your soul. In a world blessed with endings, there is nothing more you can ask for.

Lingering Threads

What of the unresolved and unresolvable? The threads of life you wish would close, lingering with no apparent end in sight. These emotions and grudges corrupt and poison you if you are not careful in seeing to their resolution. When the world does not seem to grant you an ending, you must either see to the ending yourself, or let go. Some threads you may have the choice to close out in a single day, like abandoning your pent up resentment or talking out your angers. If left to linger, these threads can be of life-changing detriment, a life-long burden of your own making that could have been resolved in an instant. Some threads may not be closable, the opportunity having either passed or existing in an uncertain future. Ignoring these threads may be the only alleviation you will find. Letting go can feel ruthless or grossly insufficient, but the cost of postponing an ending in a world that thrives on endings is deadly. Thus, the better you get at cleansing lingering threads, the lighter your burdens will be, and the easier it will be to accept new threads.

A World Without Endings

The abomination of a world without endings would be both tragic and hilarious no matter the timing. Whether joyous, painful, or bittersweet, endings prevent your reality from turning into a hell where nothing would make sense and no truth could be determined. You however, live in a world with endings, where your own truths—internal and external—will be set. And, reaching the pinnacles within your existence, depends on you siding with truth.

Pinnacles

- Siding with truth -

"Predict, Shape, Sustain, Repeat."

- Hadoffy

Creation, it seems, unravels the way.

Permutations

You will look ahead and you will see countless paths. Ambiguity and complexity at every junction, tangled threads in all directions. Decision paralysis will bind you. Intervals of pause will only be illusory and in a blink the future will be the present and in a moment the present will have passed. In a life where the ocean of possibilities is unfathomably large, and your visibility into the future is heavily obscured, the only way to have some certainty in your path is to *create the objective truths that define it yourself.*

Accommodating Reality

Dealing with ever-changing conditionals and ambiguity means that definite results in your creation will be rare. But, there are ways to mitigate this uncertainty. The model is simple: Predict, Shape, Sustain, Repeat. This model is about creation at the highest level of proactivity, being proactive with your visions and goals, not just your individual tasks. Unlike an evolutionary model, which does not have any precise goal in mind, the predict, shape, sustain model takes in an incomplete vision as input, and moulds it against reality as an output. With it, you can shape your future, even if you don't fully know what you want your future to be yet.

Predict: The future guards its secrets well. Prediction is about using your current knowledge and understanding, guided by your metrics, to make considered guesses about the future of anything relevant to your visions and self. Do not overthink too much.

Shape: Reality will bend, somewhat. Shaping is about acting within the world to either make your predictions true, or to make use of your predictions coming to fruition. You may also act to mitigate the consequences of your predictions being incorrect. It takes the frame, 'For this to be true,' and attempts to make it so.

Sustain: Every endeavour starts out with optimism. Sustaining is all about testing the outcomes of your predicting and shaping, and seeing if the resultant reality is what you wanted and if you can maintain it. In short, it answers the questions: "Can you keep this up?" And if so, "Do you want to keep this up?" In this stage you will learn much about what you want your next loop to look like.

Repeat: Adaptation requires repetition. Based on the outcomes of the full loop, you refine your goals and start the cycle anew.

Agency

You cannot map out your life path and rarely will you know with precision the future that you wish to create. Despite this, Predict, Shape, Sustain, Repeat will unravel more for you than the dry fate that will be forced upon you otherwise. With it, you can maximise your agency, and side with objective truths of your own making.

"Either the world reacts to you, or you react to the world."

- Hadoffy

Initiative, it seems, drives excellence.

Operator Behaviour

Are you reactive, proactive or predictive? The proactivity spectrum of operator behaviour is a conceptual model that characterises the way you act within the world. It applies across every context from workplace behaviour, to social interactions to sport and gaming. Every individual fluidly moves along the spectrum depending on their experience, confidence and technical skill in the given context. It applies to everyone.

Reactive Operators

Reactive people generally perform below average, struggle to get what they want and may just be new to the given context—the world happens to them.

- Reacts to situations.
- Prioritises hoarding resources and action avoidance.
- Controls nothing.
- Doesn't prioritise information.
- Doesn't communicate.
- Casual and non-autonomous decision making and action.

- Resistant to progress and change—will hesitate and panic.
- Risk averse and avoidant.
- Has a scarcity mindset—won't utilise resources until it's too late.
- Doesn't ask questions, or asks "What do I do?"
- New to the context. Is untrained in the context.
- Blames others or the environment. Does not respect opponents or the environment.
- Working with them feels… irritating, can you just use a bot?

Proactive Operators

Proactive people generally perform above average, expect to get what they want and are often experienced in the given context— they happen to the world.

- Creates situations.
- Prioritises information and action at a reasonable cost of resources. Has some control.
- Steady and autonomous with accurate intuition supported by conscious thought.
- Communicates with clarity and concision, may be wary of over-communicating.
- Persistent and maintains pressure in the right context.
- Adaptive to change. Can work in bursts for leverage.
- Understands risk and trade-offs.
- Has a conservative mindset—will conserve resources for an efficient use case.
- Asks the question "What do I know and have?"
- Takes responsibility or accountability.

- Trained in the context.
- Blames themselves or the interactions of the team. Respects hard opponents.
- Working with them feels… consistent and reliable.

Predictive Operators

Predictive people generally outperform and outclass everyone by a significant margin, push the boundaries of what they want and usually own the context—they don't just happen to the world, they shape it.

- Appears to create and predict all situations and conditionals instinctively.
- Prioritises and extrapolates on information and advanced knowledge. Maximises control.
- Urgent and autonomous with near-flawless intuition towards decision making and action.
- Communicates flawlessly. Knows when to go silent.
- Relentless and overwhelms with intended pressure.
- Manages risk and leverages momentum to scale.
- Has an abundance mindset—uses resources for an effective use case.
- Asks the question "What's next?"
- Takes responsibility and accountability if justified.
- Can hold a paradox. They can see contradictions and not have the need to combine or resolve them.
- Trained with extreme breadth and depth in the context.

- Doesn't blame anything, ruthlessly adjusts. Respects all opponents and environments.
- Working with them feels… hard to keep up, you're getting carried.

Top Tier

While you will shift along the spectrum based on experience and context, aiming for the predictive tier is the ideal:

Reactive < Proactive < Predictive

To move towards a predictive mindset, focus on:

- *Technical Skills:* Mastery within your domain.
- *Teamwork:* Synergising with others effectively.
- *Positioning:* Strategically setting up for advantage.
- *Passives:* Taking advantage of things that happen anyway.
- *Relationships & Politics:* Understanding social dynamics.
- *Finesse & Momentum:* Optimising efforts and compounding.

Advantage

Your life starts out railroaded, shaped by external controls like parents and institutions. The world just happens to you during these formative years—you get little chance to create your own advantages. But, to get what you really want, you must break this early conditioning. You must make the world respond to you. When you learn to act predictively with initiative, you side with the truths that create the advantages necessary for performance.

"Work with and battle against the human condition, to allow for true expression."

- Hadoffy

Richness, it seems, builds connection.

Unity

You will meet souls from all over, each bound to their own fate. Some will be free of burdens, others will seek solidarity. Some will seek greatness, and others will be happy in their degeneracy. You at times will feel you have nothing to add to the potent concoction of characters that enrich you. You would be wrong.

Connection

The connections you have with others profoundly shapes the quality of your life. To best connect with others, you must understand others deeply and allow others to truly know you. The greatest purity in your interactions can only happen when you express your thoughts and feelings genuinely, but discerningly

Fragility

The fragility of the human condition, including your own condition and the conditions of others, can make it impossible to express yourself truly. You and all others are susceptible to altering your external self in many scenarios, especially in reaction to the unique expression of others. Often it is the potential for consequences, even unjust, that make you want to conform, or not conform, to the people around you. Human fragility can even make true expression dangerous to you and your goals. Fragility and your own condition must be managed. There are three tiers:

- *Ignorant:* An obtuse but mostly true version of the individual that does not integrate with society. Ignores the fragility of others.

- *Conformed:* Lacks genuine expression because the individual accounts for conditions of others too strictly. Results in repulsive rigidity because they ignore their own condition.

- *Thriving:* Integrates their true self with others. Skilfully works with the varied and dynamic fragility of others and has a sophisticated understanding and control of their own condition.

Improving

There are many ways to improve your ability to battle and work with the human condition, including your own. Here are few:

I.   Be mindful of your imagination. It is powerfully misleading.
II. Humans will attack threats. Be a source of security.
III. Lean into your own tropes. Do not undercut your values.
IV. Do everything you can to understand another. This above all.
V.   Carry the light. See passed the veil and show no judgment.
VI. Beware of insecurities. They only matter if you make them.
VII. The most enriching approach to existence is to side with your own subjective truths and share them. You *will* find others.

"Alignment guides your narrative true."

- Hadoffy

Congruency, it seems, conducts the best evolution.

Internal Contest

Your life story will be anything but boring. In its narrative you will seek out much, and many things will come to you. There is much you will do, and much you won't do. Many things will not play out the way you expect. You will seek vengeance and find it rarely profitable. You will be betrayed and still welcome back your betrayer. You will take things personal and resolve to compete at your own detriment. You will lay out contingencies on contingencies and still succumb to chance. You will do all these things and more because a thought, feeling or action won out against all its valid contestants. It is only when these contestants align, when your thoughts match your feelings and your actions, that you will come to play out your most authentic existence.

External Contest

Alignment is having clarity of, and congruence with, all parts of the self, driven by your values and conditions. But, if you are to believe yourself a literal monster—a complex clump of chemical compounds responding to stimuli—then nothing matters anyway and you may blame your fate on your soulless biology. If you believe yourself to act with at least a modicum of free will, then you will struggle with finding alignment amongst endless external influences. Your calculating mind will believe it sees false patterns. Your fragile body will give in to physical strain and your character will be placed under social and parental pressures. When you allow the conventions, powers and pressures of the world to direct your choices too strictly, you may never find alignment. You become lost and purely consumptive—a husk of a human—existing but not living. An artificial monster of sorts. Your long term narrative that comes from this will never be authentic.

Broken Narratives

You must seek alignment of the self and follow it at all costs. As much as is possible. The consequences of denying your congruence are too great. Imagine a movie where the script has no constraints, no emotional direction and there is no pacing or timing defined. Scenes would be confusing, plot points would not make sense and motivations would be impossible to decipher. The movie would be an abomination. When you live without following your alignment, you are making a similarly broken narrative out of your life. Looking back it will hurt to watch. You will see your actions deviate from your true thoughts and feelings. You will have lived out nothing but a lie. The only perpetrator: you.

Imperfect Alignment

The complexity of existence makes finding perfect alignment impossible. But, striving for it gives you the best chance of siding with a life narrative true to the objective and subjective truths that make up who and what you are, and what you will evolve to be.

"Sometimes you need to stay in the lift a moment longer than expected."

- Hadoffy

Persistence, it seems, leads to ascension.

Holding On

Good things take time. Whether it be moments in the micro, or ages in the macro. There will be times you need to hold on for a few more seconds, and times you will need to grind something out over years. The times in which you must persist will be longer than you expected. Your endeavours will always be met with unexpected resistances—new reasons to give up hope or give in to fear or your lack of discipline. In these trials your patience will not always save you. You will need steadfast conviction and comparable desire, or you will not have the strength to endure.

Resistance in the Micro

In the micro, resistances manifest rapidly and will take you by surprise. These resistances are a blessing. Your most memorable moments will come from the times you blast through a resistance in the micro. It is one of the few times you will get to see really how far your skills have come. In the counter instance where you barely scrape through, you will feel a rush of excited relief like no other. If nothing in the micro was ever to go wrong, your smooth existence would grow boring and void of great stories.

Resistance in the Macro

In the macro, resistances manifest both rapidly and slowly. They appear as the accumulation of doubt or the growing consequence of sacrifice. When you sacrifice over the long term for something great, you will be in the slow part of the exponential curve of progress for a very long time. Before you begin to see an ounce of success, you will see nothing or very little in return for your efforts. It is in this period where the rewards of your sacrifice will not be clear, and your doubts will urge you to revert to comfort. To combat this ailment, you must learn to balance a tough duality. You must remain focused and grounded, while also keeping your driving fantasy alive—the overly ambitious vision and goals you have in your head. Beyond your fantasy, you need to make your sacrifices count. Rather than mourn your expenditures, let them remind you why you paid the price in the first place. All things have a price, and when your convictions and desires are correct, you will find with time that what you paid was not as valuable as what you gained. In this way, the macro can transform you such that some of your earlier resistances will no longer matter to you.

Coming in Clutch

Consistency paired with intensity, and fundamentals paired with nuance will break most of your resistances. Yet, you will inevitably be forced into a clutch moment. A time where you must execute almost perfectly, or hold out against overwhelming pressure. In this mayhem, a tiny shift in intensity or holding out for a fraction of a second longer can make all the difference against expectations. When given this choice, always side with holding out for truth.

"It doesn't matter how the dice roll, it matters that they're rolled."

- Hadoffy

Detachment, it seems, harnesses the intangible.

The Dice

To reach the pinnacle outcomes of your existence, you will have to roll the dice. You will have to take chances that terrify you. When you take a chance, you influence the outcome by making wise choices and having great skill. But ultimately, no matter what you do, the outcome is going to be what it is—the dice are going to land the way they do. Sometimes outcomes will be most favourable. Sometimes disappointingly average. And sometimes the worst possible. The one thing that matters more than any other, is that you roll the dice on that outcome in the first place.

Indifference

Every outcome is the culmination of thousands of your choices and thousands of external factors you will never comprehend. The better you get at something, the better you get at shifting the odds that the thousands of tiny details add up in the way you want. But, when you care too much about the outcome, you will adopt the damaging tendency to cling too tightly to elements you cannot control. Unless you have loaded your dice beforehand— making the perfect setup—it serves you no benefit to fixate on the uncontrollable aspects of taking a chance. These uncertainties can lead you into never rolling the dice at all, denying any chance for luck to strike. Outcomes do matter, and there are ways to increase your odds of success, but only ever acting on certainties will severely limit your existence in cruel ways that do not become evident until it is too late to amend your choices. The solution is found in stoic teachings—ruthlessly focus on what you do control. And then keep rolling the dice on that which you truly care about.

Managing Odds

With time being your most expensive resource, there is a certain urgency in life to get things right. While you can never guarantee an outcome, there is much you can do to manage your odds:

- Know when to have backup plans. Know when to not.
- Respect the gamble. Know when downsides are very real.
- Seek reference experiences. Learn to handle consequences.
- Bend arbitrary and harmless rules. Think for yourself.
- Maintain high standards and always aim for excellence.

Play it Out

Every moment of your existence is unique. Most things, even those that are repeatable, can only happen once. At any time though, if the uncontrollable can severely impede you, the inverse is true too. Luck can favour you greatly. It is absurd how often you will pull off some insane bullshit to win despite an overwhelming disadvantage. Thus, when given the chance to roll with limited downsides, always side with possibility, don't look at probability.

"Forever the truth."

- Hadoffy (Ascendant Motto)

Verity, it seems, conquers all.

Seeking Truth

With time, much is revealed to you. The decisions that bound you. Your early mistakes. Your tragedies. False truths you hold so dearly will be slowly eroded by reality. You will struggle to be free of them while better truths hide eternally. Your expectations of your future will be theatrical. The foundations of your past will be unbalanced. The calamity of your conclusion will be inevitable. Despite this unveiling with time, no matter what choices you make or what path you seek, you will never reconcile the countless competing truths forced upon you. You must seek truth anyway.

Truth Conquers

Truth is a conqueror. Brutal and dualistic in its nature. It permeates all aspects of your path, performance, social life, self, perseverance and spirituality. It is not often what you want it to be. It can be dark and hostile, uncaring for your desires or your sense of self. It is not often what it appears to be. It can be commingled out of two opposing, yet valid realities awaiting your subjectivity to give it form. These natures of truth make it terrifying to face. But, when you deny it, particularly your own, it *will* find you. And it's better to be on its side when it does.

Path

On your path, your internal truth—the unique qualities and beliefs you hold—will determine how you handle the objective truths you face. For some, structure and planning is the way. For others, chaotic and free-flowing principles are the way. Whether you are seeking to fulfil a multitude of deep intended purposes, or are simply pursuing infinite arbitrary goals, your path will always be a reflection of how your internal truths met objective truths. This clash between you and reality is convoluted. There are times you will be lost and directionless. Times you will fear the obscured way forward. What then, unravels the way?

Creation

On your path, truth is mutable. You can harness it, manipulate it, shape it for your objective goals and desires. This mechanism is your way forward. No matter who you are or what internal truths you hold, the most infallible approach to pathing is creation— bringing into existence new objective truths that make your future more like what you want it to be. Creation need not be limited to valuable products or memories. It can be relationships, fun or entertainment. When you choose to create, your next moves will always reveal themselves. Creation, then, unravels the way.

Performance

In your pursuit of excellence, truth delivers consequences. When there is contest for what outcome will come to be, the line between victory and defeat is so very thin. To shift the needle favourably such that consequences delivered by truth are positive, you must find guidance in paradigms. This creates a meta-challenge. How do you know which paradigms to apply? The choice between conserving resources or going all in. Being bold or being reserved. Being urgent or being patient. Simplifying at the cost of nuance or maintaining complexity at the cost of clarity. You can only know these answers through practice combined with theory. You will also find that your internal truths will shift what paradigms work for you, and which do not. There are times you will pick wrong. Times you cannot win no matter which paradigm you choose. What then, drives excellence?

Initiative

In your pursuit of excellence, there is a standout and all powerful paradigm that shifts truth favourably without failure in all instances: taking the initiative. Whether you are all-in oriented, brutish, simplistic and unrelenting, or precise, fast, yielding to doubt but clinical, being the first actor seizing any and all advantages will always improve your odds that the result is favourable. When you take the initiative, you minimise room for time, disadvantages or the controllable to defeat, outplay or evade you. Initiative, then, drives excellence.

Social

Within connection, truth exists as a brutal duality of beauty and horror. You and all others love the comfort of half-truths. Mostly the half-way part that is beauty, while ignoring the horror that may never see the light. Yet, that which stirs you—chaos, tension, stress, jealousy, competition, turmoil, distance, loss—these are the brutal horrors you will face in your deepest most intense connections. In them, you will have both love and fear in balanced amounts. A complementary duality that you must not let stifle you. The friends you make on your path, the others you are bound to, impact all aspects of your life so profoundly that to deny them is to deny the shared truths that precipitate the pinnacles of your existence. These shared truths may not be purely positive. There are times that your contrasts and conflicts will be disheartening. Times you will feel inexplicably lonely despite the presence of others. What then, builds connection?

Richness

The best part about the confluence of subjectivity—the creation of shared truths—is the mayhem that comes from individual truths being expressed fully and authentically, bringing richness to the concoction. Whether you are good, evil, shy, obnoxious, or any other messed up combination of self and personality traits, bringing your true personality and character fully into interactions without a veil is the optimal condition for finding shared truths that mean anything. This condition is entirely natural and primes you and others against monotony. Richness, then, builds connection.

Self

In your evolution, truth is always in conflict. Your existence is not harmonious. You are relentlessly barraged with contradicting thoughts, feelings and influences. There will always be something disrupting your sense of harmony. A pull in a certain direction. The need to push away from something close. A haunting unease sitting within your subconscious. Do not ignore your disharmony but do not let it control you. When you let disharmony fester, instead of actioning it in calmness, you stay the same, a shadow of an advanced self. To resolve your disharmonies, you must evolve. You must grow yourself into a being capable of surmounting that which ails you. But, no matter what you do, when you resolve a disharmony, another will take its place. This eternal state of being in disharmony is an ideal, not a curse. It enables you to evolve in perpetuity. This raises questions. If your final self will always be undecided, in which direction do you choose to evolve? What then, conducts your best evolution?

Congruence

The same conditions that create your need to evolve, are also the conditions that show you the way in which to evolve. Your internal truth and all its external influences will always be in conflict and there will always be disharmonies greater than the others. Target your strongest, most painful disharmonies. You do not have to resolve them fully, you only need to evolve to bring them closer to congruence with all other parts of yourself. If a belief is holding you back, remove it. If you don't like your environment, change it. If you feel your subconscious begging you to ask the difficult question, ask it. Do not look too deeply for answers outside of yourself. Stop looking for external confirmation on the choices you should make. Simply seek congruence. In perpetuity, this is the optimal mechanism for choosing the direction of your development. Congruence, then, conducts your best evolution.

Perseverance

When striving, truth is yet to be resolved. It is your heartless and enduring combatant. The only valid test that tells you that you can move beyond. On the climb, unresolved truths will contest you again and again. You will petition them for the right to proceed, and they will invite you to see that you are worthy. These unresolved truths care not of the outcome. They become the outcome. They take the form of your resolve. You either give up and defeat becomes truth, or you persevere and your success becomes truth. There are many possibilities. You will fight battles where victory is a known impossibility. You will follow wishful illusions that spur on your endurance into certain failure. You will need to cut your losses and live to see another day. With all of these possibilities and more, what then, leads to ascension?

Persistence

If you do not meet your permanent death, your contest with unresolved truths will carry on whether you like it or not. The matter becomes not about winning every contest, but making it through, no matter how many and how brutal the contests. You must persist. It is in the insane and dark times where all the best stories are written. It is in the mayhem and chaos of great obstacles where all pinnacle outcomes are found. History does not care for the person that scuttled by, existing but not striving. It looks to those that endured the most preposterous contests. Those that endured against darkness and brutality no matter the odds. Persistence, then, leads to ascension.

Spirituality

Within the intangible, truth is imperceptible. It exists as a force that can only be known to the omniscient. It is where the whisper of fortune rests in secret. It is brutal truths awaiting to be told. To master the intangible is impossible. Its complexities surpass your human limitations. Whether you look to the divine, your faith, science or philosophy, the message is the same again and again. The choice is always yours. And when you suffer at the hand of your own choices, you will begin to believe life, or the divine is against you. In your low spirit, you will lose the ability to make use of the unseen. What then, allows you to harness the intangible?

Detachment

It is through detached, deliberate action or inaction that you are granted the means to make use of the intangible. As the German proverb goes, "Begin to weave, and the gods will give the thread." When you act deliberately with detachment, you harden the spirit to withstand the brutality of truth. You still care for things. You just never allow an outcome, or expectation, to destabilise you. In this, you grant your spirit the poise to see and make use of the hidden boons that arise on your path—the lucky opportunities aligned to your goals. Detachment, then, harnesses the intangible.

Pinnacles

Truth will always win. It will demand you embrace its duality and brutality, punishing your defiance in ruthless ways. To reach your pinnacles then: *it's better to be on the side of truth, than in its way.*

Epilogue

"Existence is a game of questions."

- Hadoffy

Existing lightly.

Questions

In your existence you will have endless questions. If you go out into nature and ask your god or the universe to give you answers, you will be met with silence. If you ask a friend, a stranger or a voice in the dark, you will eventually have more questions. If you cross paths with another who is both an angel and a devil, you will be forced to see which of your own answers will hold, and which will not. Existence is a game of questions. And your perspectives will determine how you find and judge your answers.

Temporary Views

The grand difficulty of the game of existence, is that there are infinite perspectives to hold, and no way of knowing which will matter most. No matter how many perspectives you gain, there will always be a counter view around the corner, ready to challenge the one you just accepted. Whether you commit to the views of the ancient stoics, or dabble in the new age of modern data-driven thinking, there is always going to be a perspective that feels optimal and final to you… until it's not. Your choice in this matter only heightens the freedoms of this game. At any time you can change your view and how you play.

Choices

The choice of which perspectives to hold is always yours. They ultimately determine how you choose to play out your existence. You may choose to play serious and on the world stage. You may choose to play with ferocity or you may choose to play gently. Whatever you choose, in the theatre of your life there will be pleasant and painful moves. A right way and a wrong way with respect to what outcomes you could desire at any moment, including potential for grave consequences. Still, all you can do is play, doing what you can to reach the pinnacles of your existence.

Greater Choices

Your most tormenting regrets will come from failing to have the right perspective in the time you needed it. It is therefore not enough to hold a singular perspective. You need a vast and dynamic view of reality. You will need to explore. In this search you will seek guidance from others and question their validity. You will agonise over every angle and question your own self. You will see that no singular perspective captures all and rarely is your view flawless or universal. Here, at the extent of your vision of reality, you will inevitably miss perspectives your view did not allow you to see. For this reason, some of the best perspectives are the ones you will never get to see at all. And even when you have the correct perspectives, you may still not apply them willingly. This leads to a conclusion that is less uplifting and more of a warning: exist lightly. Playfully. With unbound perspectives. The alternative is to suffer a limited existence, with lesser choices.

The perspectives you hold.

- Hadoffy

Internal truths.

From the following four words, put them in order of what you naturally prioritise and value most. Think hard about what you lean towards, it can be very close between words, and different contexts will sometimes have a different ordering, so try to think holistically about your life and how you tend to act.

Another way to think about this is to consider that you have all four satisfied. When all four are satisfied, which do you seek more of?

There is no science here, it is purely an exploration of one's own perspectives.

— —

Challenge
Possibility
Stability
Connection

— —

Your *top two* words determine your ethos:

Challenge + Possibility   = Conqueror
Possibility + Connection   = Expressionist
Stability + Connection   = Nurturer
Connection + Challenge   = Unifier
Challenge + Stability   = Solver
Possibility + Stability   = Innovator

Your *top three* words determine your nature:

Challenge + Possibility + Stability = Conqueror + Solver + Innovator = **Shaper**

Challenge + Possibility + Connection = Conqueror + Unifier + Expressionist = **Storyteller**

Challenge + Stability + Connection = Solver + Unifier + Nurturer = **Master**

Possibility + Stability + Connection = Innovator + Expressionist + Nurturer = **Experimenter**

Finally, combine your ethos and your nature.

Thinking about who you are, do the words accurately match your own beliefs about how your perspectives drive you?

Acknowledgements

- Hadoffy

Finding Perspectives.

There was a precursor to this book.

Two hundred more pages.

Four times as many words.

Convoluted thoughts and streams of consciousness strung together in disjoint paragraphs with flawed structure.

It had to change.

Only through the perspectives of others was this book able to come to be the way in which its forerunner was intended.

Thank you all.

Including those gone.

And all still here.

Contact: Hadoffy@hadoffy.com

Hados | Haffy
~ Hadoffy ~